THE ECONOMICS OF PUBLIC ISSUES

THE ECONOMICS OF PUBLIC ISSUES

FOURTH EDITION

by
DOUGLASS C. NORTH
University of Washington
ROGER LEROY MILLER
University of Miami

HARPER & ROW, PUBLISHERS
NEW YORK, HAGERSTOWN,
SAN FRANCISCO, LONDON

This book is printed on recycled paper.

Special Projects Editor: Mary Lou Mosher
Project Editor: Renée E. Beach
Designer: Michel Craig
Production Supervisor: Kewal K. Sharma
Compositor: Maryland Linotype Composition Co., Inc.
Printer and Binder: The Murray Printing Company

THE ECONOMICS OF PUBLIC ISSUES, Fourth Edition

Library of Congress Cataloging in Publication Data

North, Douglas Cecil.
  The economics of public issues.

  Includes bibliographical references and index.
  1. Economics.   2.   Industry and state.   I.   Miller,
Roger LeRoy, joint author.   II.   Title.
HB34.N6   1978   330.9'73'092   77-12791
ISBN 0-06-044851-2

CONTENTS

Preface

PREFACE

Economists cannot tell people what they ought to do. They can only expose the costs and the benefits of various alternatives so that citizens in a democratic society can make better choices. In this book we present the interested reader with some ideas of what the costs and the benefits are for various proposed social actions. Economic issues surround us in our daily lives, in our work, and in our play. Often, we may not even be aware of how much economics is really involved in the public issues that we face. But they exist nonetheless, whether we are talking about abortion, illegal drugs, crime prevention, higher education, or professional sports.

For students first taking an introductory economics course, we can offer this book as a supplement to the main text. Reading it in conjunction with a book that goes into detail on economic theory can demonstrate both the relevance of that theory and the way in which it can be used to analyze the world around us. No a priori knowledge of economics is necessary for understanding any of the chapters in this book. Necessarily, then, the reader must be warned that in no case is our treatment of a topic exhaustive. We have merely attempted to expose the bare economic bones of some aspects of the issues treated. Further class discussion will, undoubtedly, reveal the more complex natures of those issues.

For professors using this book, we have prepared a short Instructor's Manual which we think is useful. It contains a lecture outline of each chapter, graphical explanations, questions for additional thought and discussion, and selected references. It is available from the publisher on request.

In this edition, we have made a number of changes and added some new materials. The new chapters include those on "The Economics of Juries," "Crime and Punishment," "The Big Apple," "Imposing a Tax," and "Saving our Cities." In addition, we have made substantial changes in the chapters on safer products, raising less corn and more hell, medical care, professional sports, the automobile, land use planning, bribery, and education. We hope that we have made changes in this edition which will more accurately reflect the issues of our times.

A number of individuals have helped us through the years by commenting on specific versions of this book. They are as follows, in alphabetical order:

Thomas Borcherding
Judith Cox
John Allan Hynes
Robert J. Lampman
John McGee

We also cannot go without thanking the numerous users of this book who have offered their suggestions for changes and revisions. We continue to welcome such comments.

Douglass C. North
Roger LeRoy Miller

THE DYNAMICS OF PUBLIC ISSUES

THE ECONOMICS OF
THE POPULATION EXPLOSION

People may not reproduce like rabbits, or even in the geometric ratios which Thomas Malthus, that dismal forecaster, predicted. But historically, the number of the world's inhabitants has tended to outstrip the available food supply. And when that number has pressed too hard on available resources, either famine or pestilence has succeeded in diminishing the world's population. At least that was the case until modern times. During the past 200 years, the situation has changed, especially in those parts of the Western world where man has climbed to an unprecedented standard of abundance. More surprisingly, this change has been achieved during a period of phenomenal population growth. The world held a population of roughly 730 million inhabitants in 1750 and of more than 2.5 billion a century later. Now, about 4 billion humans walk this planet. Have we, nonetheless, finally emerged into permanent abundance, or is this merely a utopian interlude, at least in the United States?

The easiest way to understand this issue is first to look at the centuries prior to 1750, and then to compare the situation of the modern world. During the centuries of chaos that followed the decline and fall of the Roman Empire, the number of people in Western Europe appears to have decreased. Then, from approximately the ninth century until the end of the thirteenth, population grew in that region. Another reversal came in the fourteenth century, beginning with a severe famine between 1315 and 1317 and compounded by the nightmare of the Black Death, which swept over Europe for the first time between 1347 and 1351. The plague became endemic to the Occident, raging again and again in the next century, so that population declined absolutely for at least a century. Then another cycle of growth set in (about 1470–1580) followed by at least stagnation if not an absolute decline (1580–1680). Since then, population has grown continuously, although the rate did not begin to accelerate until the last half of the eighteenth century. (Currently the rate has decelerated in many parts of the world.)

This growth pattern can probably be explained by the same factors which for many millennia must have determined the number of inhabitants on the earth. The crucial and interrelated elements are: (a) the size of population; (b) the techniques (tools, equipment, knowledge) which people have at their command; and (c) the land and resources available to them. Technical knowledge grew relatively slowly during the first 1700 years after Christ. If we look at the population of Western Europe in the ninth century in relation to the land available, it is evident that vast parts of Northwestern Europe were sparsely settled or even in a state of absolute wilderness. As population grew in particularly favored areas, the amount of land per person of course decreased, and not even the additional labor available could maintain the previous per-capita supply of food. But that was no cause for concern, since anyone who felt crowded or deprived could simply move out to the unsettled frontiers. On this basis, colonization of Western Europe continued for centuries. Even lacking any improvement in technical knowledge, the additional population could produce as much as their predecessors because of the abundance of rich virgin land. During this period, therefore, the output of foodstuffs, as well as of materials for clothing, housing, and other necessities, at least held at a constant amount per capita. There came a time when this situation changed. By about 1200 all the best land in Western Europe had been taken up, and *constant returns* gave way to *diminishing returns*. An additional peasant now had either to work the existing cultivated agricultural land more intensively than before or to move onto what proved to be poorer land. In either case the amount of foodstuffs (and other raw materials) that individuals could produce was less than that of their predecessors. Between 1200 and 1300 the continued growth of population resulted generally in diminishing returns (to additional labor effort) and a progressive fall in the standard of life of the peasantry. Weakened by malnutrition, they were easy prey first to famine and then to pestilence. Once the latter had become embedded in the environment, it continued to make inroads long after the populace had declined to levels that left a good deal of excellent land vacant.

Whether the plague gradually petered out or the surviving peasantry built up some degree of immunity to it, population began to grow again. A second cycle of growth and diminishing returns occurred between 1450 and 1680. But there was a difference which made the second decline far less deadly. Not only had migration to the New World become possible, but new techniques were available, allowing greater production per individual than before. As a result, Western Europe escaped from the recurring cycle of Malthusian disasters. Population continued to grow but output grew even faster, so that rising living standards on a sustained basis became a reality.

Today, the world's population approaches 4 billion, and it could amount to considerably more by the end of the century. Few virgin lands are left, and their innate fertility is, with exceptions, not likely to be high. But it is not only sheer numbers of people that give an accurate guide to the rate at which resources are being gobbled up in advanced countries; it is also the income and rate of consumption of each person (relative to his or her ancestors or to people in poorer countries). For example, in 1960 in the United States, the per capita consumption of crude oil was 700 gallons (for automobiles and heating); bituminous coal was 4000 pounds (converted to electricity or used as an input in manufacturing); steel was 1100 pounds; salt was 300 pounds (only a small fraction of which was for seasoning).

It is not surprising that a new generation of Malthusians has emerged to warn us that we are headed toward mass famine or, at the very least, toward the end of an era of spendthrift abundance. After all, the size of the earth is limited; so we do have a fixed factor. Sooner or later we will have dug up all the minerals, siphoned off all the oil, and stretched the capacity of agricultural lands until the food supply can increase no more, or can do so only at the expense of using a prohibitively greater percentage of our labor and capital. We shall examine this issue in Chapter 2. In this chapter we shall look at the demographic aspects of the problem, where the rate of population growth is a function of the rates of birth and death.

While both birth and death rates have responded to economic changes, the triumphant decline of mortality in the past two centuries accounted for much of the population growth. Anyone who considers the modern city polluted would be appalled by the unsanitary conditions of its counterpart of even a century ago. When rising living standards were coupled with the application of improved sanitary and medical knowledge, the decline in death rates, particularly among infants, became a potent factor in population levels.

However, it is not to the mortality rate but to the birth rate that the civilized world must turn for control of population size. Fertility has responded in some degree to economic conditions even before modern contraceptives were devised. In earlier centuries, periods of famine and declining income were countered by delaying the age of marriage and by primitive forms of birth control (sometimes even by infanticide). However, with the development of modern and efficient forms of contraception and the widespread practice of illegal or legal abortion, fertility (or lack of it) has become a deliberate decision for many. At least in developed countries, whether to have children and how many to have, are regarded as decisions to be arrived at by rational choice on the part of the family unit.

In the agricultural world of the past centuries, children were, for their parents, as much an investment as a source of enjoyment. On the farm a child could probably "pay his way" by age eight, and the family farm essentially recruited its labor force from within. Moreover, since children were counted on to care for aging parents, an "extended family system" served as a form of social security. As we would expect, therefore, fertility rates in agricultural societies were high. In the United States until very recently, farm families were much larger than city families, and in developing nations large families are considered an economic safeguard.

Why do urban couples have children? They are certainly not a good investment economically. From birth they require large expenditures on which no "returns" of gratitude, much less of income, can be confidently anticipated. Parents have children for their own enjoyment. That is to say, in economic terms, that children are a consumption rather than an investment good; moreover, the economic costs of this consumption good have been rising substantially. The Institute of Life Insurance has estimated that the median-income family must spend $75,000 raising one child until age eighteen. On top of this amount, one must add the income forgone in rearing a child rather than being in the labor force. The more human capital (skills) the person who raises the child has, the greater the income forgone. Since parents usually support their children throughout their years of schooling, for the most part, and since the costs of education have been rising relative to other goods and services, children have been growing relatively more expensive. We would expect, therefore, in the absence of a change in people's tastes in favor of children rather than other consumption goods, that fertility would decline as an ever-growing portion of Americans becomes urbanized and is faced with the rising cost of raising and educating children. And that is precisely what is happening. Fertility among whites is at one of the lowest levels in our history; if the present trend continues, the white population will have a zero rate of population increase in another decade or two.

It appears that economic considerations do indeed affect fertility rates. If that is correct, and we wish to use these incentives to reduce fertility, then we should keep in mind that proposals to establish family allotments according to the number of children (as provided in some countries) would appear likely to increase fertility. Even the modest deduction of $750 per child permitted under our present federal tax law acts in that direction, for that matter.

If we truly wish to reduce birth rates, the means are at hand. They would take the form of dissuasive tax incentives—that is, tax rates increasing with the number of children. We are not suggesting that this is the only course of action, or an appropriate one. It is merely a possible way of reducing population growth once a country has decided that the optimal population has been reached or will be in the near future.

THE ECONOMICS OF
INCREASING SCARCITY

Just a few years ago, a group of scientists with the aid of the
MIT computers came up with some startling projections outlined in the Club of Rome report, *The Limits to Growth:* Our
exponentially increasing consumption of the earth's finite resources will exhaust reserves far sooner than most of us would
imagine. Well, it does appear that scarcities, and increasing
ones to boot, seem to be cropping up throughout the world in a
frightening number. Let's look at one of the most pressing potential crises that is being predicted by the experts—diminishing food supplies.

Table 1 shows that the so-called index of world food security
fell dramatically from 1961 to 1974, when the number of days
of reserves, as a share of annual grain consumption, dropped
from 95 to 27. Indeed world carry-over stocks—that is, the
amount of grain or food in storage at the time a new crop
begins to come in—have fallen precipitously in the 1970s.
World consumption of grain has been expanding at 2.5 percent
annually, but carry-over stocks have not kept pace and by
1975 are estimated to be less than a month's consumption. In
other words, working reserves have dwindled while consumption has continued to climb.

7

Table 1 *Index of World Food Security*

Year	Number of Days Grain Reserves
1961	95
1962	88
1963	77
1964	77
1965	69
1966	66
1967	55
1968	62
1969	69
1970	69
1971	51
1972	66
1973	37
1974	27
1975	21
1976	25
1977	?
1978	?
1979	?
1980	?

Source: U. S. Department of Agriculture, and L. R. Brown and E. P. Eckholm, "Food and Hunger: The Balance Sheet," *Challenge,* September-October, 1974, Table 1, 18.

Some experts have contended that there are only three lines of action that can be taken in order to draw the world back from the edge of a food crisis precipice: creation of a world food bank, the modernization of agriculture in the poor countries, and an intensification of agricultural and food research.

The idea of storing food now is not at all new, but it has increased in popularity as experts and lay persons alike increasingly believe that famine is just around the corner. A significant number of magazines and newspapers carry the ads of companies selling storable food that can be kept in basements or other storage places just in case of famine.

The same type of analyses and similar recommendations to prevent the world from dropping over the precipice of a petroleum crisis have also been proffered. It has been shown that, at current rates of production, we will run out of our reserves of petroleum within a very short number of years. In fact, according to D. H. Meadows et al., the authors of *The Limits to Growth*, it is most probable that we only have 20 years' supply of petroleum available in the ground.[1] Even if we use a static index in which there is no account taken of exponentially growing demand, the reserves will only last 31 years. Given that the authors of the study firmly believe exponential growth is implicit in our system, the number of years' reserves of other nonrenewable natural resources seems frightening indeed:

Resource	Years' Reserves
Aluminum	31
Copper	21
Lead	21
Mercury	13
Natural Gas	22
Zinc	18

We could go on and on about different critical areas of increased scarcity in our world today, but the analysis would be essentially the same. The question then remains: Will the purported increased scarcity change our way of life? According to many observers, in our new era of scarcity it will be disastrous for individuals to engage simply in economic laissez-faire; that is, individuals will no longer be able to go about life simply in the quest for personal gain. Such behavior and indeed democracy as we know it are considered by some to be the luxuriant

[1] With more than three million copies in print the Club of Rome Study continues to have a tremendous impact on public opinion. In the meantime, in response to widespread criticism by economists, the authors in a new report have changed their mind and are far less pessimistic about future shortages and pollution.

fruits of an era of apparently endless abundance. As the economist Kenneth Bolding has pointed out, we live in the spaceship earth, which means that when we reach its outer limits, our behavior must change. Other economists have come up with even more far-reaching predictions about the future: " . . . an orderly response to social and physical challenges will require an increase of centralized power and the encouragement of national rather than communal attitudes. The voluntary abandonment of the industrial mode of production would require a degree of self-abnegation on the part of its beneficiaries—managers and consumers alike—that would be without parallel in history."[2]

Yet the historical record—right up to the present—does not lend much support to this self-denying view. At the time of the American Revolution approximately 90 percent of Americans worked in agriculture. By 1929 the figure was 22 percent, and at the present time it is less than 5 percent and still falling. It is not just the percentage of people in agriculture that is decreasing; the absolute number in agriculture is also on the decline. In 1910 the U.S. farm population consisted of 32.1 million people. By 1967 it had fallen to 11 million. In 1820 each farm worker produced enough food and fiber to support four persons. Today he supplies forty persons. In addition, the amount of land in agriculture has fallen absolutely from 365 million acres in 1929 to 308 million acres in 1967. During this same period, the total of crops raised on this land increased 50 percent and livestock (and livestock products) increased by 86 percent. In short, despite an absolute decline in farmland and labor, agriculture is producing vastly more than it did in earlier times.

But we don't need to rely on these general figures. Detailed studies of the production of individual agricultural, mining, and forest products usually show declining labor costs per unit of output between 1910 and 1960. In effect we are moving in the reverse direction from that predicted by latter-day Malthusians.

[2] Robert L. Heilbroner, *An Inquiry into the Human Prospect* (New York: Norton, 1974).

What is the explanation for this situation? Partly, it exists because the amount of nonrenewable resources in the earth is staggering in magnitude. In the case of minerals, for example, one reputable expert has estimated that if the earth's crust were a perfectly homogeneous mass with minerals distributed uniformly, each cubic mile of rock would hold a billion tons of aluminum, 625 million tons of iron, and so forth, down to the relatively scarce minerals—650,000 tons of copper, 185,000 tons of lead, and 60 tons of gold. However, since minerals are more concentrated, the amount of the earth's surface already mined is still a miniscule fraction of the potential. A second explanation is that when diminishing marginal returns have set in for a resource, the resultant rise in price has tended to encourage a search for substitutes to replace it and superior means to produce it, that is, technological change. But the overwhelming reason (which stems in part from the second explanation) is that technological advances have occurred at such a rate that increases of supply at all prices have outrun the parallel outward move in the demand schedule. There are undoubtedly other costs, not included here, which are by-products of this exploitation of resources; but for the United States, the plain simple fact is that we are not running out of resources, as that term is usually conceived.

To the present, this increase in man's productivity has outstripped the growth of population in many countries. Whether it can continue to do so depends on: (a) whether man can discover technologies to overcome diminishing returns, (b) whether the side effects of man's exploitation of the environment will destroy him, and (c) changing fertility and mortality rates.

It is important that we do not confuse short-run crises with long-run increases in relative scarcities. We have faced a petroleum crisis, a wheat crisis, and a fertilizer crisis just as in various earlier years since World War II we faced meat crises, soybean crises, and so on. But we should note that these were short-run crises generated by cartel agreements, crop failures, and so forth, and that the resultant rise in price has set in motion the market forces to correct the problem. This confusion by neo-Malthusians in which every short-run scarcity has been projected into a perpetual shortage can do nothing but lead to misguided policies. This does not mean that we should not be concerned about the long-run dilemma. We have no assurance tnat technological developments will always bail us out or even that panic responses to short-run shortages may *perpetuate* them into long-run shortages. All we can say is that an increasing relative scarcity of resources is not evident at this time.

3

THE ECONOMICS OF
ABORTION

Very few of the major issues of our time are purely economic, and abortion is no exception. An economist is in no way qualified to answer the pivotal question of whether life begins at conception, at 24 weeks, or at birth. Nor can an economist summarily state whether or not abortion should be legally permitted or proscribed. Pregnancy termination was practiced in ancient times, and any prosecution associated with abortion seems to have been based on the father's right to his offspring. English common law allowed abortion before quickening (when fetal movement is first evident); it is doubtful that abortion after quickening was considered a crime. The American colonies retained this less restrictive English common law until the changeover to state statutes at the time of the Constitution. In 1828, New York enacted an antiabortion statute that was to be a model for most of the other states. The statute declared that abortion before quickening was a misdemeanor and abortion after quickening second-degree manslaughter. In the late nineteenth century, the quickening distinction disappeared, and the penalties for all abortions were increased.

In 1967, thirteen states had reformed their abortion statutes in partial conformity to recommendations of the American Law Institute and the American Medical Association. Little by little, states started to ease the conditions under which it was legal to perform an abortion. A landmark Supreme Court decision in 1973—*Roe* v. *Wade*—overruled all state laws prohibiting abortion before the last three months of pregnancy. At that time it was thought that the controversy over the legality of abortion had been settled. However, the Supreme Court's ruling in many ways has spawned more questions than it has answered. There had been, by 1977, numerous amendments to the Constitution introduced in Congress, all of them seeking either to ban abortion on demand entirely or to leave the question of abortion up to the individual states. While we cannot go into the merits and demerits of the legal issues here, we can examine some of the economic consequences of legalization.

The performance of any abortion, except in extraordinary circumstances, was long a criminal activity in the United States. Therefore, it is impossible to obtain accurate figures on the number of women who have undergone the operation, the percentage among them injured as a consequence of unsanitary abortion conditions, or the mortality rate. Nevertheless, some crude estimates point up the magnitude of the situation.

In New York in 1970 before the legalization of abortion, it was estimated that a qualified doctor charged about $1,000 for the illegal operation. On Canada's west coast the price was approximately $500. Before the U.S. Supreme Court's ruling in 1973, more than 350,000 women were admitted annually to American hospitals with complications resulting from abortions. Finally, it is estimated that more than 1000 women a year died from improperly performed pregnancy terminations.

Even allowing for a very large percentage error in these estimates, it is clear that illegal abortion was, for a long time, big business, and that the number of women who undertook both the risk of criminal prosecution and the danger of crippling infection or death is substantial.

Let's begin by looking at the economics of illegal abortion, the situation that long prevailed in this country. Who was willing to perform the illegal activity and at what price? A doctor convicted of performing an illegal abortion faced not only criminal prosecution but also expulsion from the medical profession, and the consequent lifetime loss of license and livelihood. In addition he or she may have had to endure ostracism by a community which regarded abortion as a criminal act. In short, the costs to a doctor of such a criminal conviction were immense. Yet, in many communities there were doctors whose strong moral convictions made them willing to bear these risks. Reputable doctors performed abortions every day; and those who did not were sometimes willing to refer patients to other physicians who would take these risks (at a price). Many, perhaps most, pregnancy terminations were, however, performed by unlicensed abortionists under unsanitary conditions. The referral was often by word of mouth from, say, the local hairdresser. It was apparent that varying numbers of people, both qualified M.D.'s and less qualified lay persons, were willing to perform illegal abortions. The number and proficiency of those available differed according to the prices women were willing to pay.

At the top of the scale—perhaps $800 to $1000—was the licensed physician willing to perform the illegal activity at a price which compensated for the recognized risk. Below that were doctors for whom various admixtures of moral values and risk determined the price. A few with strong moral conviction would perform the operation for only $100–200. But most abortionists asking a price that low were unlicensed, poorly qualified practitioners whose product could hardly be guaranteed. A rating scale would have shown relatively few licensed M.D.'s willing to perform abortions at the $100–200 level with the number growing as an increased price tended to compensate more adequately for the risk.

The illegality of abortions, of course, increased the costs of both supplying and obtaining information, as we will show is also the case with euphorics. Information is never free, even in legalized activities, since it costs money to acquaint potential buyers with the location, quality, and price of a good or service. But in the case of an illegal activity the providing of information is even more expensive. Abortionists could not advertise;

and the more widely they let their availability be known, the more likely they were to incur arrest. While some doctors unwilling to perform an abortion did refer patients to other, more lenient M.D.'s, the referral was itself illegal and therefore risky. There were other ways of obtaining information about the professional competence of an abortionist, but how reliable is the local hairdresser? The high cost of information had its effects: Women seeking an abortionist were not able to inform themselves of all the possibilities without spending lots of time and some money.

Contrast these conditions with those that existed after abortion became legal. Information is no more costly to disseminate or to obtain than it is for other medical specialties such as pediatrics or dermatology. Specialists can be listed in the classified section of the telephone directory and with the county medical association. Anyone seeking a specialist can consult these sources or ask any physician for a referral.

Once the risks associated with illegality are removed, what governs the price at which a doctor is willing to perform a legal abortion? The M.D. who charged $800 for the illegal operation will no longer command that high price, since other doctors will now be willing to perform the operation for less. But how much less? We can get some idea if we see how physicians value their time while working. Suppose a doctor agrees to perform an appendectomy during a busy week. He or she may charge perhaps $100 for spending an extra half-hour doing it. If, instead, the doctor chose to perform an abortion which would also require a half-hour, he or she would not be earning a fee for removing the infected appendix. The foregone earnings for the half-hour spent in performing the abortion instead of the appendectomy amount to $100. *Opportunity cost* has thus determined the value of the service, and he or she now has some idea of how much to charge for the abortion.[1] This basic determination does not, of course, include any special

[1] This assumes that competition among doctors would force the price to this level. For a qualification of this point as well as an examination of what determines doctors' opportunity costs, see Chapter 12, "The Economics of Medical Care."

equipment or facilities. When legalizing abortions, some states have stipulated that they must be performed in a hospital. This requirement obviously substantially raises the price to be paid. To the doctors' opportunity costs must then be added the charges for hospital facilities utilized during the half-hour, which could perhaps mean $150 added to the cost of a pregnancy termination.

This simplified example by no means indicates that a single supply price can be expected to prevail among all doctors for performing legal abortions. The quality of a doctor's services varies according to his or her training, experience, and innate ability. But even given this consideration we should note that the overall relationship between the quantity of abortions supplied by M.D.'s and the price they are paid to perform the operation is different after abortion is legalized. It is still true that doctors will perform more abortions at higher fees because the increasing size of the reward induces them to forfeit doing other things. But at any particular fee, there will be more M.D.'s willing to perform the operation when it is legal than when it is illegal, because the risks are removed. Note also that the quality of the service would in general be higher, since nonqualified practitioners will have little place in the picture with the operation fully legalized.

Let us turn for a moment from the supply of legal abortions to the demand for illegal ones. The potential "buyer" of an illegal abortion faced a whole range of prices for the operation. Which would be chosen (i.e., what was the *demand schedule*)? Three simple examples show the process of decision.

The wife of a rich executive visits a travel agency which arranges a package tour to Japan. Included is round-trip air fare, an operation by a doctor in that country where abortions are legal, and three days subsequent sightseeing. The price tag: $2000.

Next let's take a look at how the wife of a young lawyer earning $20,000 a year resolves her dilemma. She goes to her doctor; on the quiet the doctor refers her to an M.D. willing to perform an illegal abortion for $600.

Then, there is the situation of the wife of a blue-collar

worker making $8000 a year. Surreptitiously asking around, she finds out from a worldly acquaintance that the local barber will do the operation in a back room for $200, aspirins included.

If we investigate the relative numbers of women in each of the above categories, we discover a definite pattern in which the costs and risks of acquiring information were important elements in each woman's decision. Only a few could afford and were willing to incur the expense of the Japanese tour; progressively more could and would pay the intermediate price; and many women seeking abortions felt that only the lowest price was within their reach.

It is easy to see how the costs of information could be prohibitively high for a woman at the lowest level of income. She is probably not the patient of a top-rank doctor who could refer her to a safe abortionist. If she arrived unreferred at the office of a highly placed obstetrician, it would be unlikely that this doctor would take the risk of referring her to anyone he or she knew. Friends to whom she might turn were no better supplied with reliable information than she was.

It is not surprising that mortality from abortion appears to have been inversely related to income. Better information was more available, with a correspondingly smaller risk, as the income level rose. We have seen that a woman's inability to uncover reliable information could lead her to choose dangerous alternatives in which she ran a high risk of crippling infection or even of death.

The statistics for New York City in the early 1960s support the plausibility of this argument: Private hospitals aborted one pregnant woman patient in 250; municipal hospitals, one in 10,100. The rate for whites was five times that for nonwhites and thirty times that for Puerto Ricans. Obviously, lower-income women were not having as many abortions performed by qualified M.D.'s in hospitals as were upper-income women.

Under legal abortion, information costs are drastically reduced, since the prospective patient has only to ask her physician or consult the ads in the classified section of the daily newspaper. Moreover, when abortion carried the stigma of criminal activity, many women were unwilling to have the operation even if they did not want the child. By removing the stigma, legalization resulted in a substantial increase in demand even at the same prices as before. But what actually did happen to prices after legalization?

It has already been shown that illegal abortion was offered at not one price, but many depending on the quality of service, information of the patient, family connections, etc. The situation can be contrasted with the pricing of, say, an agricultural commodity such as wheat. At a moment in time, there is only one price quoted *for a particular kind and quality* of wheat. The essential information is known to all traders because all transactions are carried on in one central location: the Board of Trade in Chicago.[2] No such coordination existed in the case of illegal abortions. The quality of the product ranged from the skills of a highly experienced Japanese or American doctor to the haphazard methods of a back-alley quack. Such a wide range of qualifications could exist only because of the curtailment of the spreading of information to everyone involved. The result was, in effect, a whole series of separate situations arising from the unique conditions imposed by illegality. Even in the case of legal abortions there are variations in price and quality, although they are fewer and far less extreme. However, the "standard" price in the long run is clearly much lower under conditions of legality.[3]

If, however, a state insists that abortions be performed only in a certified hospital, as the 1973 Supreme Court decision held that it may after the first three months of pregnancy, an illegal market will continue to exist. The additional hospital fees will keep the "standard" legal price well above that which low-income women can afford or are willing to pay. In such cases, back-room opportunists will very probably continue to provide

[2] Almost 90 percent of the noncommunist world's grain is bought and sold through one central location—the Chicago Board of Trade. These brokers have easy access to price and quality information for most parts of the globe.

[3] And even lower if there were free entry into the medical profession.

illegal abortions at the "right" price. As long as a quack's opportunity cost plus his subjective evaluation of the risk involved is less than the price of a legal abortion, a market for the illegal service will exist.

Whatever might be the theoretical analysis of the legalization of abortion, the actual facts of the matter are now clear. One finding shows us that in 1969, 6524 women were admitted to New York City's municipal hospitals with medical complications following abortion. That number declined to 3253 during the year in which the Supreme Court legalized abortion. A study that appeared a few years ago concluded that "it appears that legal abortion depressed overall fertility, but particularly illegitimate fertility, by giving women an opportunity to terminate their pregnancies when other means of birth control either had not been used or had failed. . . . legal abortion prevented large numbers of illegal abortions from occurring. Our data indicate that well over half—most likely between two-thirds and three-fourths—of all legal abortions in the United States were replacements for illegal abortions."[4]

[4] June Sklar and Beth Berkov, "Abortion, Illegitimacy, and the American Birth Rate," *Science*, vol. 185 (September 13, 1974), pp. 914 f.

4

THE ECONOMICS OF
EUPHORIA

Marijuana is illegal; so are hashish, mescaline, dimethyltripta-
mine, psilocybin, and tetrahydracannabinol. The illegality of
these drugs does not, of course, prevent their use by young and
old alike. It does, however, add certain peculiar characteristics
to their production, distribution, and usage.

Before we look at drugs, we can learn a few things by examining an historical experience that proved unforgettable to
most who lived through it—Prohibition.

On January 16, 1920, the 18th Amendment to the United
States Constitution became effective. It prohibited the ". . .
manufacture, sale or transportation of intoxicating liquors
within, or the import into, or export from the United States for
beverage purposes." The Volstead Act, passed in 1919 to re-
inforce the 18th Amendment, forbade the purchase, possession,
and use of intoxicating liquors.

A once-legal commodity became illegal overnight. The results were impressive, but certainly could have been predicted
by any economist. Since the legal supply of liquor and wine

fell to practically zero[1] and much of the public continued to demand the commodity, substitutes were quickly provided. Supplies of illegal liquor and wine flowed into the market. Increasing quantities of whiskey clandestinely found their way across the border from Canada, where its production was legal.

Of course, fewer entrepreneurs were now willing to provide the U.S. public with liquor. Why? Mainly because the cost of doing business suddenly increased. Any potential speakeasy operator had to take into account a high risk of being jailed and/or fined. He also faced increased costs in operating his bar, for the usual business matters had to be carried on in a surreptitious—i.e., more costly—way. Moreover, the speakeasy operator had to face the inevitable: an encounter with organized crime. He could look forward to paying off organized crime in addition to the local cops. Payments to the former reduced the possibility of cement shoes and the East River. Payments to the latter reduced the probability of landing in jail.

As a general summation it could be said that Prohibition probably decreased the amount of alcoholic beverages that entrepreneurs were willing to provide *at the same prices as before*. If a bottle of one's favorite Scotch was available for $3 in 1919, either it would have cost more in 1920, or it would have been filled with a lower-quality product.

Whiskey lovers faced another problem during Prohibition. They could no longer search the newspaper ads and billboards to find the best buys in bourbon. Information had gone underground, and even knowledge about quality and price had suddenly become a much dearer commodity. In general, consumers have several means of obtaining information. They can find out about products from friends, from advertisements, and from personal experience. When goods are legal, they can be trademarked for identification. The trademark cannot be cop-

---

[1] The exception was wine intended for religious purposes. The use of so-called sacramental wine increased by 800,000 gallons in the two years following ratification of the 18th Amendment, leading to interesting speculation about whether Prohibition somehow made Americans suddenly more religious.

ied, and the courts protect it. Given such easily identified brands, consumers can be made aware of the quality and price of each via the recommendations of friends and ads. If their experience with a product does not jibe with their anticipations, they can assure themselves of no further encounter with the "bad" product by never buying that brand again.

When a general class of products becomes illegal, there are fewer ways of obtaining information on product quality. Brand names are no longer protected by the law; so falsification of well-known ones ensues. It becomes difficult to determine which trademarks are the "best." We therefore can understand why some unfortunate imbibers were blinded or killed by the effects of bad whiskey. The risk of something far more serious than a hangover became very real.

For some, the new whiskey-drinking costs were outweighed by the illicit joys of the speakeasy atmosphere. But other drinkers with more sensitive ethics were repelled by liquor's illegality and were deterred from consuming as much as they had before Prohibition, even if it had been obtainable at the same price as before.

While it is difficult to assess the net effect of these considerations, one fact is clear. The impact of Prohibition differed between the rich and the poor.

High-income drinkers were not particularly put out at having to pay more for whiskey of the kind they wanted. They ran little risk of being blinded, because neither the high price tag nor the cost of obtaining information about quality and supply could separate them from their favorite beverages. Presumably they would have been quite willing, before Prohibition, to pay more than the going price.

On the contrary, some lower-income imbibers had probably been paying just about their top limit for whiskey of acceptable quality before Prohibition. The sudden rise in costs left them two alternatives: Do without or settle for less, in the form of bootleg booze and bathtub gin. The distribution of injury, sickness, and death due to drinking contaminated whiskey directly mirrored the distribution of income.

The analogy is obvious between what happened during Prohibition (The Noble Experiment) and what is now happening with respect to most euphorics and hallucinogens. Like bootleg liquor, these drugs share the stricture of illegality which leads to both relatively high costs and high risk in their manufacture, distribution, sale, and consumption.[2] Yet there is a difference between the two periods in the matter of who obtains the more-wanted product. The wealthy user still is able to buy quality; he or she may even pay intermediaries to do the necessary shopping around. But while the middle-income user ends up getting inferior drugs, the "heads," or high-consumption users, who are also poor, probably often get hold of the better-quality euphorics, and often at prices below those paid by others. The reason for this situation involves a mixture of economics and sociology. First, these people would not be poor unless they were working at low-paying jobs—if they are working at all. Therefore, when they spend time away from their jobs, not much is lost, and we say that the opportunity cost of their not working is low compared to those with higher-paying jobs who must sacrifice more earnings when they choose not to work. The poor user merely responds to the low opportunity cost when he or she spends more time seeking out the best buys in the urgently wanted drugs. This was true during Prohibition, also, but it didn't have as much import because there was not then such a large sociological class of "heads" devoted to the whiskey "cult."

On the other hand, the problems that face a middle-income drug user are manifold. If this user spends time seeking out information about which euphorics to buy and where to find them, he or she is confronted with higher opportunity costs for time spent away from work. Potential jailing is a greater deterrent in terms of both opportunity costs and psychic and emotional costs. And since this individual is probably unable or unwilling to pay some intermediary to do the necessary searching (as the rich user would do), he or she ends up with drugs of a quality that would be scorned by many low-income "heads."

A parallel, and a question, might be found in the case of

[2] Although a number of states have in many ways "decriminalized" the use and possession of small quantities of marijuana.

abortion operations. We noted in Chapter 3 that many rich women fly to Japan to have legal abortions performed. Since the use of certain drugs is quite legal in other countries, why don't rich users fly overseas to obtain and use their drugs? Take the case of Nepal, where high-quality marijuana can be purchased for about 2 cents per ounce, while the price in the United States might run as high as $40 for the same quality and quantity. The relative price of the Nepalese euphoric is thus 1/2,000 that of the U.S. euphoric. Or is it? When we consider the *total* cost, we see that we must include round-trip air fare to Nepal, plus the opportunity cost of the flight time (minus any monetary value placed on seeing that exotic country). The relative price of one ounce of legal Nepalese marijuana now becomes more like $\left(\dfrac{\$.02 + \$800}{\$40}\right) = 20$ times the U.S. price for illegal marijuana.[3]

Up to now we've been dealing mainly with the demand side of the illegal drug picture. We have looked at the determinants of how much people buy and how much they are willing to pay for a certain quality of euphorics. Now let's look briefly at the supply side. We wish to find out what determines how much people are willing to furnish of a certain quality of euphoric at different prices. The parallels to be made with the supply of whiskey during Prohibition are numerous. The illegality of the manufacture and distribution of most drugs poses a large risk to suppliers. The risk is higher the greater (a) the probability of detection, (b) the probability of conviction, and (c) the potential jail sentence and/or fine. Costs of doing business include measures to assure secrecy and avoid detection, payoffs to organized crime (for certain drugs not easily manufactured, like heroin), and potential payoffs to the police.

What would happen if marijuana were legalized? Should we expect a general state of euphoria?

On the supply side, entrepreneurs would be able to supply

[3] The added cost to the user of detection, conviction, and jail are, of course, not included in the $40 price for U.S. euphoric. However, the probability of detection and the costs of conviction are sufficiently low in the United States so as not to induce anyone to pay 20 times more for the pleasure of smoking marijuana in Nepal without fear of arrest.

larger quantities at the same price as before because the costs of doing business would fall. There would be no risks involved, no requirement for payoffs to organized crime, and no high cost of maintaining secrecy in production and distribution. The price of many drugs would eventually fall to a level just covering the lower costs of legal production and legal distribution. In fact, we could even get more *cannabis* supplied if we were to repeat what happened in the colonial period. Then the English parliament established a bounty to encourage American planters to produce hemp. At that time *cannabis sativa* was a valuable article of American commerce. The seeds were used for oil, and the stalks of the plant could be fashioned into webbing, twine, bagging, and rope. The hemp fibers added durability to any material with which it was interwoven. The crop was important enough for King James I of England to declare it illegal for any settler who had hemp seeds not to plant them!

When there is unrestrained competition among the sellers of a legal product, it is difficult for relatively inferior products to exist side by side with better ones unless the price of the former is lower. Otherwise sellers of the superior product will inform the buying public of the anomaly. Since the product is legal, the free flow of information will assure that some buyers will refuse to purchase inferior products unless their price is correspondingly lower.

By opening the door to advertising, legalization would also reduce the costs of disseminating and obtaining information about supplies. Competition among sellers and increased information available to buyers would combine to raise the quality of the product.

On the demand side, legalization would, of course, reduce to zero the threats of detection, conviction, and jail, with their attendant costs. Because of higher overall quality, the risk of bad side effects from improperly prepared drugs would be lessened. Both of these cost reductions would lead consumers to demand a larger quantity even at the prices which had prevailed before legalization.

It is difficult to predict whether the price would rise or fall immediately after legalization. Since consumers presumably would demand more, suppliers would produce more. If the increase in demand were to exceed that in supply, a shortage would be the result and consumers would find themselves paying high prices to obtain as much of the now-legal product as they wanted. In the long run, however, it could safely be predicted that prices would, as usual, fall to a level just covering the costs of production, distribution, and normal profit—which would certainly be lower than the price paid today. (In fact, given world-wide availability, we can safely assume that the supply of drugs in the United States is highly elastic at the approximate cost of production.)

If drugs were to be legalized and this chain of events occurred, one more link in the sequence would be a fall in the price of euphorics relative to that of alcoholic beverages. Would this lead to a trend away from drinking—and toward the smoking of marijuana, for example? The answer hinges on an "if." If marijuana is a *substitute* for alcohol, this might well happen. But if the two are *complementary* instead of substitutable, then increased use of marijuana would lead to increased use of alcohol.

In any event, the above analysis does not constitute an argument for or against legalization of euphorics. There are costs to society involved in each course. There are also benefits. Describing the costs of making something illegal does not necessarily argue for a change in the law. After all, there are costs involved in passing a law which forbids wife abandonment, but society obviously has decided that the benefits of making abandonment illegal far outweigh them.

THE ECONOMICS OF
SAFER PRODUCTS

Coke bottles that explode in people's faces. Electric can openers that electrocute. Rotary mowers that amputate the hand of the operator. Nightgowns that burn their wearer to death. Cars that crash without warning because they are put together wrong. . . . The number of product-related accidents is staggering. The cost of these bizarre mishaps is even more so, for the lost income of those injured, maimed, and dead as a result of fateful purchases mounts up fast. Recently there has been a movement to protect consumers against unsafe products. In fact, the Consumer Product Safety Commission has been functioning for some time now. Its job is to oversee the level of product safety in the United States—to guarantee, presumably, that people will not bear any "undue" risk when they drive their cars, mow their lawns, or drink a beer. To analyze the effectiveness of legislation to improve product safety, it might help to look at the level of safety that would be dictated in an unrestricted market situation.

Let's take the example of an electric toothbrush manufacturing firm. Suppose it is the first one to enter the market. How does it decide how safe to make its toothbrushes? It would be nice to think it will make them absolutely safe, but absolute safety is impossible, but if it were, it wouldn't come free of charge. Making a product safer usually involves a higher cost of production, and that usually results in a higher price, which in turn lowers the quantity demanded. Our electric toothbrush manufacturing firm probably knows this. At first, it has no information on what level of safety the public demands, so it might arbitrarily pick one. Let's say that one buyer in 50,000 gets electrocuted. This, of course, raises the true cost of the toothbrush to all users because of the probability of their suffering egregious harm some morning when they can't even see clearly into the bathroom mirror.

Now suppose another manufacturing firm comes along and believes that that level of safety is insufficient. This firm wants to make an electric toothbrush that will electrocute only one in every 150,000 users. Its cost of production may be a little bit higher, but it advertises that its product is safer. If it is correct in assuming that the market demand for safety is greater than that actually provided by the first toothbrush-manufacturing firm, it will end up getting a larger share of the business. The first firm will have to follow suit if it wishes to compete; otherwise it will eventually go out of business.

In fact what probably would happen is that some consumers would prefer a cheaper even if somewhat less safe product and others would prefer a more expensive one with greater safety. As a result, as the electric toothbrush market expanded there would be different submarkets with different price/quality combinations reflecting consumers' subjective tradeoff between price and safety.

This, then, is the mechanism by which the level of product safety desired by the public is discovered by manufacturers. It is a trial-and-error system that is not completely accurate at any point in time because information is never perfect. The key aspects of this argument are that the level of product safety will be demand-determined—that is, determined by the buyers of the product—in this particular situation, and that competition among producers will indeed result in the so-called optimal level of product safety.

But this optimal level of safety assumes that all consumers are informed about the risks that they take and can make a rational decision about the price/safety combination that they desire. But we know that information is not free. As such products become more complex and more numerous, the costs become significant and the consumer becomes more bewildered. This is the rationale for government safety regulations. Let's see how they work in the case of the automobile.

The automobile is the product that has had the most legislation with respect to its safety or lack of same. Safety legislation was instigated by the discoveries Ralph Nader exposed to the world in 1965 in his book *Unsafe at Any Speed*. He later testified at Congressional hearings. Congress and the President were adequately impressed to pass legislation setting up the National Highway Safety Bureau, later renamed the National Highway Traffic Safety Administration. Most people are aware of the numerous regulations that automobile manufacturers must now follow: dual brakes, double-laminated glass, no interior protrusions, over-the-shoulder seat belts, soon-to-be-required airbag passive restraint systems, and so on. We have no doubts that new automobiles are safer than they would be in the absence of such legislation. The occupants of these automobiles will sustain fewer injuries than they would have otherwise. We are talking here, however, only about the supply side of safety for automobiles. The supply of new automobiles is indeed safer. But the price of new automobiles is higher too. Let's see why by looking at the costs of making a Hornet or a Chevette.

There are certain costs that the manufacturing firm must incur no matter how many or how few of a new-model car it sells. These costs include, initially, those of design and marketing research to determine what will sell best. Once the decision is made to produce a certain model, the costs of tooling up—that is, making new body dies, jigs, features, and new engine tools and molds—must be considered. Then follow all the costs of setting up the production line for the new car. And, if the new model is to be accepted by the public, it has to be introduced via promotion—i.e., TV ads, billboards, and radio commercials—all of which involve costs.

All of the above are called *fixed* or *"sunk"* costs. Once they have been incurred by the auto manufacturer, they are gone forever, whether the car is bought by 100 people or by 100,000.

In addition to these costs, there are others which vary according to the number of cars produced, the most obvious being for labor and material inputs. The more cars that are made, the more labor-hours are required and the higher the manufacturer's total wage bill. And the more cars made, the more steel used, the more upholstery bought, the more steering wheels ordered, thus the higher the bill for total materials. Costs in this latter group are called *variable* because they fluctuate with output, although the relationship need not be one to one.

In addition to all this, we must realize that the car company has to make a profit or go out of business. In a competitive industry and in the long run, the rate of profit for one firm is usually not much higher than for any other, although differences obviously exist.

It seems difficult, however, to classify the auto industry as competitive when one examines the profits of General Motors relative to Ford, Chrysler, and American Motors, or even relative to the average for all manufacturing firms. There have been numerous explanations for GM's rather remarkable capacity to make relatively high profits. One of these involves a phenomenon known as *economies of scale,* or more familiarly, *gains from mass production.* This means that when GM doubles *all* its inputs, its output more than doubles. Thus the larger its production, the smaller is its average cost per unit. By producing millions of cars, GM can charge the same price as other companies while clearing higher profits on each car sold. But we are left with a question: Why doesn't GM lower its prices below their present level (for it would still be making a profit) and eventually capture a larger and larger share of the market until no other company exists? We suspect that if GM really enjoys the reputed economies of scale, the reason it fails to act this way and drive all other makers out of business is the looming potential of an antitrust suit. GM does not want to be broken into bits as was Rockefeller's Standard Oil in 1911.

What, then, determines the price we pay for new cars? In the *short run* each company will make the most money if it ignores sunk costs (letting bygones be bygones). It should sell cars up to that number at which the revenue from selling an additional automobile will not cover the costs of producing it. The price which gives a company the biggest profits will be about equal to the costs involved in making that hypothetical final car.

We all know, of course, that no car maker is likely to figure things out by the slide rule of this analytic procedure.[1] We also know, however, that in the *long run* the manufacturer has to cover all costs and earn a "reasonable" profit or the owners will go into another business where they can make more money.

What, then, is the implication of this latter statement in the matter of required safety features? It is simply that the costs of such amenities will, sooner or later, be paid by the consumer. Seat belts, collapsible steering columns, and dual braking systems require additional resources. Somebody must pay for them, and eventually the tab will be picked up by the buyer of the car, although the manufacturing firm may share the costs if it is earning more than a competitive profit to start with.

Government regulation of safety features on cars has already raised the price of cars higher than it would have been otherwise.[2] Unless the quantity of cars that people demand is totally unresponsive to changes in the price, when the price goes up, fewer cars will be bought. Some families will have fewer cars, or will trade in their cars less often, or will depend more on taxis, buses, and trains.

---

[1] We can predict behavior using this theory, though, even if the individual decision-makers do not reason this way.
[2] When *marginal costs* are increased, so, too, is price.

Since imported cars are a substitute for American-made ones, U.S. companies have had every interest in prodding Congress to impose federal safety standards uniformly on *all* cars. Otherwise the relative price of imported automobiles would have fallen and more people would have bought them than before, at the expense, of course, of domestic car sales.

Whether more lives have and will be saved with the existence of, and compliance with, federal automobile safety standards is, however, a subtle question. When a greater amount of safety is supplied, some individuals will drive less carefully. The economist's standard model will then predict that individuals driving in less safe cars would drive more carefully; individuals driving in more safe cars would drive less carefully.

Using such a model, Professor Sam Peltzman finds that there is some empirical support for such predictions because: (1) more than a proportional share of automobile accidents occur with cars that have safety equipment in comparison to those without it, (2) there has been an increased amount of risk-taking by drivers, as evidenced by an increase in the amount of drunk driving, and (3) the percentage of auto-related deaths accounted for by pedestrians has increased, relative to auto occupants (who have safety equipment).[3]

We note, for example, that during the period in which safety devices have been required on cars, the number of accidents has increased while the number of deaths of auto occupants has not. These data are again consistent with the view that individuals may be driving more recklessly because of required safety devices on their cars.

One of Peltzman's conclusions is that legally mandated automobile safety devices do work to save certain lives, but their efficacy has "created forces which have dissipated their life-saving potential."[4]

---

[3] Peltzman, Sam, "The Regulation of Automobile Safety," in H. G. Manne and R. L. Miller, Editors, *Auto Safety Regulation: The Cure or the Problem?* (Horton: Glen Ridge, New Jersey, 1976).
[4] Ibid.

Further, even if this risk-taking effect were minimized, we must still realize that safety improvements are not free. Increased safety requires the use of real resources, and thus raises a fundamental issue which cannot be resolved here, but which we should think about. Suppose the new safety standard saves 100, or even 1000, lives a year at an additional price of, say, $50 million in costs to the consumer. Is it worth it? At some price we can make every car a tank and completely safe for its occupants. Since very few people would care to pay the price of a tank, such an expedient might also solve some problems of pollution and congestion, but it is doubtful that the idea would meet with overwhelming enthusiasm from consumers. In fact, if they were offered a tradeoff of various increasing degrees of safety in their cars but at successively higher prices, we would probably find that a great many people would not opt for higher levels of safety. Most would be willing to accept additional risk in trade for a lower-priced automobile.

Note, however, that we have removed this alternative from the consumer. The choice of the price/safety combination which would result from the market forces discussed at the beginning of this chapter has been replaced by a uniform minimum level. The demand for safety has been imposed rather than consumer-derived. Moreover, this minimum level keeps rising as new legislation is passed each year.

It is perfectly clear that we do indeed place a price value on life, even though such an idea seems objectionable. At some price we can obviously eliminate automobile accidents, but we do not choose this solution. Where, then, do we draw the line?

Each individual makes some decision on the value of his or her own life when he or she decides whether to take a train or drive a car, whether to work in a dangerous occupation (at relatively high pay) or to work in a safe one (at lower pay). Most people say that a human life (especially their own) is "priceless." Human behavior today does not support this statement. Do you spend all of your resources in preventing any possibility of accident?

Of course, there still exists an argument for imposing safety standards, even if drivers must pay more for their cars. Certain drivers' actions can affect others who have no say in the matter. If a driver has poor brakes, he may run over pedestrians who may never be fully compensated for their injuries. Thus safe brakes are required on all cars. Note, however, that this argument does not apply to padded dashes, for example, which protect only the car's occupants.

6

THE ECONOMICS OF
IMPOSING A TAX

By now you should be able to deal in a quite straight-forward manner with the economic consequences of imposing a tax. The results, at first glance, are very similar to what we observed in the chapter on the economics of safer products; that is, a tax on an industry's output will often shift the supply curve to the left by the amount of the tax with a result that it will both push up the price of the good and reduce the quantity offered for sale. Thus as in the case of safer products, the effect is on the supply because the higher tax decreases the quantity offered at every price. Take for example a tax imposed on wine of let's say, 50 cents per fifth. Will the price of wine rise by 50 cents, that is, will all of the tax burden be borne by the consumer? By now you should be able to answer this question. Clearly, the price will rise, but not by the total of 50 cents per fifth since there will also be a smaller quantity demanded (depending on its elasticity), and at the new equilibrium, the price will be higher but by less than the full 50 cents.

But if the consumer did not bear the whole burden of the tax, who did? The answer is that the winery did. The resources that went into producing the wine are less valuable than they

were before the tax. In effect the wealth of the producer has
been reduced.

So far, so good, but that's really just the beginning of the
story. The tax that we have described is what is called "per
unit" tax. That is, it is a tax per fifth of wine. Supposing that we
consider as an alternative, an ad valorem tax which would be
a tax on the price of wine. What difference does this make? If
the product in question is a unidimensional product, that is, it
is of one constant quality, with no separable characteristics, the
answer is, it makes no difference at all. But most products, in
fact, don't fit such simple characteristics. Wine, for example,
runs the gamut from Gallo Hearty Burgundy, which may sell
for approximately $1.50 per fifth, to Romanee Conti which for
a bottle of 1961 Vintage may cost up to $75.00 a bottle. Ob-
viously, there is a significant difference in quality in the eyes
of consumers.

Now let's consider the implications of the two different taxes.
A per unit tax of 50 cents a fifth is 33 percent of the price of
the Gallo Hearty Burgundy and hardly shows up as a percentage of Romanee Conti. Conversely, if the tax is an ad valorem
tax of 33 percent this will lead to a rise in the price of Gallo
Hearty Burgundy of something less than 50 cents a fifth but
may lead to a market price of Romanee Conti that may be more
than $20 higher. Thus a per unit tax has made Romanee Conti
relatively cheaper as compared to Gallo Hearty Burgundy
while the ad valorem tax has done just the reverse. We can
summarize the results of this by pointing out that a per unit
tax induces the substitution of quality for quantity while an ad
valorem tax induces the reduction in quantity and quality. The
implication of this finding suggests some quite unexpected results with respect to taxation. For example, a gasoline tax is
often regarded as a means to combat air pollution. Usually the
tax is constant per gallon so that the increase in cents per
gallon is the same for regular as it is for high octane making
the latter relatively cheaper. The result is that market substitution will induce purchasers of gasoline to buy more higher

octane gas. However, higher octane gas has a main constituent, lead, which is a major air pollutant, and thus a tax which results in higher octane gas being more preferred, could lead to an absolute increase in the level of pollution rather than the reverse which was its intended purpose. Under such circumstance, the tax would have backfired. The moral of this story is that taxes which are imposed on goods which have a number of separable characteristics may produce unexpected results. It is very unlikely that a tax will cover all of these separate dimensions of a good or service and to the extent that it fails to do so it will result in multiple changes in resource allocation away from the taxed aspects of the commodity and into increased utilization of those characteristics of the commodity that are not so taxed.

THE ECONOMICS OF
THE PERNAMBUCO
TRAMWAY

It sounds plausible. The price of gas, water, oil, electricity, housing, transport—you name it—is too high! So, set a lower price and provide a system of enforcement that prevents chiselers from getting away with illegal prices. Does it work? We might label one attempt the Pernambuco Tramway syndrome, and pass it off as a fairy tale.

Once upon a time, there was a foreign company that received a franchise to build a streetcar system in the growing city of Pernambuco, Brazil. They built the system and people rode back and forth on the streetcars. The original fare (Who can remember way back then?) was one-tenth of a cruzeiro.

It is important to note that the rate was fixed by government edict, and that the foreign company received a return on its investment equal to what it could have obtained with other uses of its funds, or maybe a little higher. (That is, it equaled or exceeded the opportunity costs of the firm's capital.) Now as time went by, the real value of the cruzeiro began to fall because inflation set in. As the beleaguered cruzeiro dropped from a cent to a half-cent to a quarter-cent, the fare—still fixed by edict—no longer produced enough revenue to cover the costs of the system. After a while it could not even cover the costs of current operations (variable costs). The company actually lost money every time a streetcar ran down the street. The company tightened its purse strings; it certainly was not going to put more money into the system. So the cars and rails deteriorated. Every once in a while a loose rail came up through the floorboards and spitted a passenger like a roast pig. Actually, by this policy of reducing the quality of service, the tramway operators were raising the real price to users, who now were paying the same fare for a service of pretty dubious value. The streetcars stood empty most of the time. When last heard from, the company was trying to curtail schedules and to sell, or even to give, the operation to the government. This is one fairy tale without a happy ending. But why worry about it?

The reason we worry is that the Pernambuco Tramway syndrome is very much with us. Prices legally held below equilibrium level are a fact of everyday life.

We face a natural-gas crisis, a garbage-disposal crisis, a water-shortage crisis, and an electricity crisis. While some of these crises also involve other problems, a major factor in each is a price set so low that the amount demanded at that price exceeds the amount suppliers are willing to offer, resulting in a shortage.

In the case of electric power, the consequences are becoming more and more widespread, as indicated by brownouts, blackouts, and sometimes rationing. In some other industries, such as transportation and water systems, the suppliers of electricity face a problem which a single rate exacerbates. The demand for their product at the fixed rate is not constant, but is subject to peak periods. In the case of electricity, the brownouts occur at these periods of extraordinary demand. On the eastern seaboard, for example, the peak demand comes during the hot days of summer when electric air conditioners are whirring. In the Northwest, by contrast, the demand peaks as a result of electric space heating in cold weather. Variations in demand are not only seasonal, but occur within a day. In some areas the heaviest use comes from 5:00 P.M. to 10:00 P.M., followed by a relatively light demand until 7:00 A.M. In short, we have an industry which has unused capacity for much of the year, and for a good part of every day, but which is strained beyond its capacity for short intervals. To be able to meet these peak demands, the typical electric utility may have to maintain so much excess equipment that it will be operating, on the average, at only 55 percent of capacity.

It is not hard to pinpoint the economics behind the problem. Under a single, uniform rate for electricity, the peak-load user is being subsidized by all other consumers, since the costs of maintaining excess equipment are shouldered equally by all users. If the power company were to adjust the single rate, charging higher prices for peak-period use than for other times, available evidence indicates that less would be demanded at the more costly periods. Peak-period use would tend to level off, while the lower price during slack periods would encourage greater use at those times. Skillful planning along such lines might effectively eliminate overloads and their resultant brownouts and blackouts.

Is such an adjustment of the single rate practical? Would it work? It does in France today. Beginning in 1954, *Electricité de France* instituted a multitariff pricing system for electricity, the different rates being set to best approximate the actual cost of supplying the additional electricity for any specific season and time of day. Because in the summer months demand is greatest during the day, a higher price is set for the daylight hours than for the night. The differential pricing also takes into account changes in sources of supply. Because winter cuts off the flow of water for hydroelectric stations, more expensive thermal generation must be used. Therefore, French consumers pay more for electricity in winter than in summer. After a careful examination of the French experience, one economist wrote that a "clear improvement over the [old] pricing scheme is very plausibly claimed."[2]

---

[2] Thomas Marschak, "Capital Budgeting and Pricing in the French Nationalized Industries," *Journal of Business* (January 1960), p. 151.

Recently, peak-load pricing for electric utilities in the United States has been strongly proposed by the Environmental Defense Fund (EDF). It was successful in getting the Wisconsin Public Service Commission to implement peak-load pricing for the first time in the United States. The EDF has presented arguments for peak-load pricing not only in Wisconsin but also in New York, Michigan, California, and elsewhere.

8

THE ECONOMICS OF
THE BIG APPLE

In our story of the Pernambuco Tramway we looked at the immediate problems of setting prices "too low." In this chapter we shall explore some other ramifications to setting prices below a market-clearing price. But this time we are examining the consequences of rent control in New York City.

Before we tell this story, it will help to describe briefly the way in which a market adjusts to changes in supply and demand both in the short run and in the long run. By the short run, we mean a period of time which is too short for the building of new housing units. Now that does not mean that the supply is perfectly inelastic. Why not? The answer is that a higher price for housing will encourage people who own homes or housing units to be willing to rent part of the units out rather than keep them all for themselves. Therefore there is some short-run elasticity of supply. A shift in demand, reflecting, as it did in New York City in war-time, a sudden insurge of people seeking apartments, would lead to a sharp rise in price and some increase in the quantity of units available.

The consequence, in the long run, is to set in motion the forces that make for a new equilibrium which is the heart of the way in which a market system works. The sharp rise in price of apartments makes it very attractive for entrepreneurs to invest their money in building new housing. To put it another way, the rate of return to investing in the housing stock has increased as compared to other ways an entrepreneur could use his capital. This results in new construction which in turn leads to a downward movement in the price of housing as the supply increases, until ultimately an equilibrium is reached. Note, therefore, that the implication is that the long-run supply of housing is relatively elastic under these conditions in contrast to the short run. The long-run equilibrium is one in which the rate of return on investing in one more unit of housing is just equal to that of investing in any other similar economic activity with the same degree of risk. Now back to our story of New York.

The federal government imposed rent control as a temporary wartime measure in 1943. While the federal program ended after the war, it was continued in New York State, and specifically in New York City. The law in the city kept rent for certain categories of apartments at fixed levels, allowing a 15 percent increase when a tenant moved out. Needless to say, an immediate consequence was that landlords tended to encourage such departures by everything from pounding on the pipes to cutting off the heat. Since there were many more people wishing apartments than there were apartments available, a longer run consequence was the development of a vast array of devices to attempt to get around the restrictions. The most obvious was what was called key money, which was a way to charge a prospective renter a large amount of money simply to get a key to the apartment, or one could hire the landlord's son to repaint the apartment at a substantial fee. In still other cases, the landlord would discriminate amongst prospective tenants on the basis of race, religion, dogs, children, or whatever. Still another consequence was that landlords simply failed to maintain apartments, so that the real cost of upkeep were decreased.

All of these policies, of course, suggest that landlords and tenants were simply finding a way to get around the artificially low price and in fact develop a de facto equilibrium. That is, the real value of apartments deteriorated and fell and/or the tenant in fact paid an extra price. Thus in reality shifts in the supply and demand curves have taken place. One obvious consequence was that there was widespread evasion on the part of everyone with respect to the law. Thus, laws were passed in an attempt to force landlords to maintain apartments, but these were widely evaded. Similarly, there were laws passed that were designed to prevent subletting for higher prices. And these too were widely evaded, so much so that a 1960 survey showed that 25 percent of renters were paying more than was legal with the rent controlled apartments. Note that this did not include bribes or cuts in quality. These were simply people paying above the amount stipulated. What we observe in such a case is that the market does find its own equilibrium.

But that does not mean that they are not significant consequences for renter and landlord. Clearly, the landlord suffers in terms of a drop in income and a renter suffers in terms of a quality reduction in apartments. But that is not nearly the end of the story. As of 1975, some 642,000 apartments were rent controlled. Another 650,000 were covered by another complex form of regulation called rent stabilization. During the whole period since World War II, there has been almost no construction of apartments that would be subject to rent control. Moreover, as apartments deteriorated because it was not worthwhile for landlords to keep them up, eventually the annual taxes on the apartment houses exceeded the income that the landlord would receive and the apartments were simply abandoned. In 1970, 33,000 housing units were abandoned. And as late as 1974, 10,000 were abandoned. In some parts of the Bronx and on Manhattan's lower East Side, whole rows of abandoned apartment houses stood gutted and stripped by vandals. Thus, the long-run consequences in New York City have been a decay in the housing stock and a decline in the amount of available space for middle and lower income tenants (luxury apartments that were exempted from rent control have continued to be built). But it has more serious consequences: The tax base of New York has been primarily based upon housing, real estate, and as its tax base eroded away, the fiscal income of New York City has declined.

The result as we all know has been a city perched on the edge of bankruptcy.

9

THE ECONOMICS OF
PROSTITUTION

In 1945, a French politician—one Mme. Marthe Richards—
demanded closure of all Paris brothels. She claimed that the
178 licensed houses, 600 prostitute-serving hotels, 10,000 pimps,
and 6000 ladies of the night were "undermining Parisian
morals and health." Moreover, she estimated that the closing
of brothels would make available 6000 rooms for students and
those bombed out of their homes during the war.

The Municipal Council of Paris, impressed by her statistics,
gave the brothels three months to shut down. The effects have
been far-reaching, to say the least, and apparently have not
proved too satisfactory, because recently a vigorous campaign
has been shaping up in France to restore the legality of the
world's oldest profession. Although the product differs considerably, the economic analysis of prostitution is similar to those of
abortion and euphoria, with, of course, a few new twists.

The service that prostitutes offer for sale has, like all others,
two dimensions: quantity and quality. In some sense, these two
are interrelated; quantity can be increased by lowering quality.
The quality of the service is, among other things, a function of

(a) experience (*human-capital investment*);[1] (b) the innate
characteristics of the provider of the services, such as looks
and intelligence; and (c) current operating expenditures such
as how much money is spent on appearance, surroundings, and
health.

To be sure, *substitution* is possible among these three aspects
of quality. Perhaps the same quality can be achieved either by
being born beautiful or by spending effort and money on
make-up and clothes. Some ladies of the night are able to compensate for poor looks by dressing well. We say that they are
able to substitute clothes for natural endowments.

For many who utilize the services of a prostitute, the health
aspect of quality is of utmost importance. The decision to
make prostitution illegal in France has notable consequences
on the probability of some clients contracting venereal disease.
Let's see why.

When prostitution was legal, numerous business establishments existed whose purpose in life was offering prostitutes'
services. Since all was on the up and up, they could advertise
without risk. Because clients could easily compare prices and
qualities, information was relatively cheap. If it became common knowledge that the employees of one house spread venereal disease to their customers, that firm would either have to
lower its prices drastically or suffer a drop in clientele.

Even though cheap information made it inadvisable for any
firm to allow unhealthy employees to work (because clients
would go elsewhere), the French government made doubly
sure that venereal disease was kept at a minimum by requiring
weekly medical inspections. Since most prostitutes worked in
establishments, it was relatively easy to check all of them, and
social disease was rare among prostitutes before 1947. The
reader can easily draw the analogy between legalized prostitution and legalized abortions and narcotic usage.

When prostitution was legal, suppliers of the service charged
their opportunity cost, with no "risk" factor added, since no

---

[1] You are making an investment in your own human capital by attending
college and by reading this book.

threat of imprisonment or fines existed. Those demanding the service had no need to invest large amounts of their resources (time and effort) obtaining information that would help them avoid the risk of a poor-quality product, as represented by the threat of venereal disease.

What has happened in France since 1947? Obviously there are no more legal houses of prostitution. The girls, for the most part, have taken to the streets. The cost of doing business has increased. Streetwalkers must avoid detection and arrest either by cleverness or by paying off police. Some girls must stay outside more than before, adding a cost of discomfort. Also, they no longer benefit from economies of scale that previously kept down the cost of such "accessories" to their trade as an attractive atmosphere. Thus, at the same wages as before, fewer prostitutes were willing to stay in the profession after 1947.[2]

On the demand side, clients could no longer be so confident about the quality of the product, because competition among legal houses was removed. Previously, any house that got a bad reputation suffered. But now individual prostitutes can more easily lower quality (i.e., have V.D.) and still obtain clients, for information has become much more difficult to obtain. And, of course, there are no longer government medical inspections. (Such a situation would be tantamount to a system of FDA inspection and labeling of different grades of marijuana in our own country.)

Predictably, as information about quality has become more expensive, the wealthy citizen has been the one able to pay the cost of seeking out the healthy prostitutes, while the poor have contracted venereal disease. If a poor woman suffers from a bad abortion, the rest of society bears little of the cost. If a middle-class marijuana user dies from some arsenic in an illegal cigarette, the rest of society bears little of the cost. But if a dock worker contracts V.D., he is not alone in bearing the cost. Other parts of society must also pay, because he can spread the disease to others. This problem explains in part why there

---

[2] The *supply schedule* shifted inward to the left.

is right now so much fervor in France about legalizing prostitution again: The rates of V.D. have soared among those associated with the prostitution industry (suppliers and demanders alike).

In summary, the prohibiting of prostitution in France caused a decrease in the number[3] and in the average quality of prostitutes, probably a decrease in the number of demanders (even at the same prices as before), and probably a rise in the average price to the customer. As an added effect, V.D. became more common among common folk.

[3] Or in the rate of growth.

THE ECONOMICS OF
RAISING LESS CORN
AND
MORE HELL

When Mary Lease stumped the Kansas countryside in 1890, she urged the farmers to raise "less corn and more hell," and that's just what they have been doing ever since.

In the late nineteenth century, their activities took the form of political campaigns aimed toward: (a) expanding the money supply, which they felt would increase agricultural prices faster than other prices; (b) introducing railroad rate regulation designed to lower freight rates for transporting agricultural products; and (c) curbing monopolies, which they felt would reduce their costs for commodities. When prices of farm goods rose at the start of the twentieth century, the farmers stuck to raising their corn, and during World War I they expanded their production dramatically in response to soaring prices. Then, after the war, European countries imposed high taxes on any agricultural goods crossing their borders. Along with other factors, this restriction reduced the amount of corn that American farmers could sell. Farm prices fell sharply, and farm organizations in the 1920s began to view their problem as one of relative overproduction. Numerous cooperative efforts were made to restrict production; but these efforts failed (except in a few specialty crops such as tobacco, where the relatively small number of producers made mutual agreement more feasible). Most crops were produced under competitive conditions: A large number of sellers (and buyers) dealt in a product which was undifferentiated (one farmer's corn was just the same as another farmer's corn). Accordingly, it was impossible for producers to organize themselves on a voluntary basis. But what farmers failed to do by voluntary cooperation in the 1920s, they accomplished via governmental directives in the 1930s. The result was a farm price-support program that was kept intact until a few years ago. What we would first like to do with this issue is examine the results of the price-support program when it was operative.

We can see the results best by first examining the market for agricultural commodities prior to price supports. In that competitive market, a large number of farmers supplied a commodity—we'll use peanuts as our example. The sum of the quantities that individual farmers will supply at various prices makes up the *aggregate supply schedule* of a commodity. Each farmer supplies only a small part of the total quantity of peanuts. He cannot influence the price of this product. If he raised his price, anyone wishing to purchase peanuts could easily buy from someone else at the going (equilibrium) price. And no farmer would sell below the going price because he would make less money than possible, since he could sell all that he produced at the going price. Thus, every unit of output farmers sell goes for the same price. The price received for the last (*marginal*) unit sold is exactly the same as that received for all the rest.

The farmer will produce peanuts up to the point at which, if he produced one more unit, its production costs would be greater than the price received. Every farmer faces the same production decision. Notice that at higher prices, farmers can incur higher costs for additional units produced and still make a profit; so at higher prices all farmers together will produce more. But again, no farmer alone can influence the price. No farmer will stop producing until he stops making a profit. That is, each farmer will end up selling peanuts at the going price, which will equal his costs of production plus a *normal profit.*[1]

The price at which each farmer can sell his peanuts depends on how people feel about buying it, and that depends on their tastes, incomes, and the prices of substitutes. The demand for food in general is quite unresponsive to price changes because there are no close substitutes. The demand for peanuts is more responsive to price changes because of available substitutes. Even so, it takes a drastic reduction in the price of peanuts to get people to buy a lot more. Conversely, an increase in unit price doesn't cause people to buy much less. (The demand for peanuts is relatively *price inelastic.*) This situation has implications for peanut farmers.

Agricultural costs of production and output can vary greatly from year to year because of, among other things, variations in weather. During a good year, production may be relatively large. But since the demand for peanuts is relatively inelastic, farmers will have to drastically reduce the price of their peanuts if they are to sell it all. They may even have to sustain a loss that year. The opposite situation occurs when production is small one year because of, say, a drought.

In sum, the short-run competitive market in peanuts resulted in changing prices of the product, changing profits for the producers.

Now how has the usual price-support program worked? The government decided what constituted a "fair price." The formula for this vital determination was the ratio between the prices farmers historically paid for what they bought compared to the prices they received for their crops in "good" years. How could the government make this arbitrary price "stick" since it was above the level that would have prevailed otherwise?[2] It agreed to buy the peanuts at that (parity) price.[3] Actually, the purchase was disguised as a loan from the Com-

---

[1] This is actually a cost to society, since it is required to keep him farming peanuts instead of changing to an alternative occupation.
[2] Called the market equilibrium price.
[3] This is one possibility only; usually the support price has been between 75 percent and 90 percent of parity.

modity *Credit Corporation* that never needed to be repaid. Historically, the government has either stored the peanuts or sold them on the world market (as opposed to the domestic market) at the going price. Since World War II, the world price has often been well below the support price; thus, the government has made a "loss." For example, in 1976, the support price for nonedible "crushing" peanuts (used for their oil), was $394 per ton, but the world market price was $256 per ton. The U.S. government has been, in effect, subsidizing peanut farmers to the tune of $50–200 million per year.

In order to prevent too much surplus, the government in 1941 allowed a maximum of 1.6 million acres to be used for peanut production. However, the yield per acre has tripled since then and the allotments haven't been cut back. Moreover, a lot of "illegal" peanuts have been grown in the past few years. That is, peanuts have been grown on land not officially allowed by the original allotment program. Since there has been as much as $165 per ton gross profit to be made by selling the peanuts at the support price, it is not surprising that some farmers have wanted to grow peanuts "illegally."

Price supports mean two things, then: (a) higher prices to the consumer for those products whose fixed (parity) price exceeds the price that would otherwise prevail; and (b) more governmental resources (taxpayers' money) expended in agriculture than would be otherwise.[4]

If it is true that price supports and acreage restrictions actually increase the wealth of farmers, there should then be every incentive for more entrepreneurs to start new farms and to share in the profits. This incipient threat of new competition was met in an interesting way by the tobacco farmers. More than three decades ago, they found a way around the problem by fostering legislation which allotted to 500,000 growers the right to raise tobacco on lands then in use. For all practical purposes no new land has been put into production since then,

---

[4] Additionally, resources were and are devoted to getting and keeping those subsidy payments; the illegal milk co-op payments exposed during the Watergate investigations are a case in point.

because a prohibitive tax of 75 percent is levied on all tobacco grown on unlicensed land.

Owners of licensed land have thus been granted a monopoly in tobacco-growing. If you were to buy some of this land today, would you expect to make money as a monopolist? If you answered "Yes," you are in for a surprise. The price of land was long ago bid up to levels that yield new owners only a competitive rate of return. The ones who made money were the original holders of the tobacco licenses, who reaped profits to the tune of $1500 to $3000 per acre ($3000 to $6000 in current dollars).[5] The same analysis can be made for owners of farmlands after price supports went into effect. One study concluded this: "Most of the net benefit of the price-support program has been capitalized into the value of farm land."[6]

Since the program for controlling tobacco production also includes restrictions on how much leaf each owner can put up for sale and at what price he can sell it, the net results have been: (a) a smaller supply of tobacco than would otherwise have been provided, (b) a higher price for tobacco than would have prevailed under free competition, (c) a consequent higher price for tobacco products.

The implications of the last statement depend on the elasticity of demand for these products. If people smoke more or less the same quantity of cigarettes and cigars regardless of relatively small variations in price (i.e., if tobacco products face inelastic demand), then higher prices simply mean that more income will be devoted to tobacco products and less to other things. Since this seems to be the case, the tobacco program has thus resulted in a transfer of income from cigarette smokers to the original owners of the tobacco-growing licenses.

[5] F. H. Maier, J. L. Hedrick, and W. L. Bigson, Jr., *The Sale Value of Flue-Cured Tobacco Allotments,* Agricultural Experiment Station, V.P.I., Technical Bulletin no. 148 (April 1960).
[6] D. Gale Johnson, *Farm Commodity Programs: An Opportunity for Change* (Washington, D.C.: American Enterprise Institute for Public Policy Research, May 1973), p. 3.

Much of what we have presented about price supports seemed to many like a purely historical lesson in the early 1970s. At that time many price-supported staples such as corn and wheat seemed to be in short supply. World agricultural prices were far above support prices. There was increased talk of scarcity and famine. Accordingly, most acreage restrictions were eliminated. A new system for the agricultural sector was put into effect a few years ago. It involved "target prices" for grains and cotton. Farmers sell their crops in the free market for whatever they will bring. If, however, average prices fall below target prices, the Department of Agriculture then pays the difference in the form of a subsidy, with the total cash payment limited to $20,000 per farmer. For at least the first couple of years of this new program, free-market prices greatly exceeded target prices so that no subsidies were paid. If at some time in the future unrestricted market-clearing prices fall below target prices, American taxpayers will again be transferring income to farmers. And, if farm product prices fall dramatically, we can probably predict that some form of price supports that were used before will be put into effect again.

We know that farmers are responsive to changing prices, not only in how they manage their own production but also in how they attempt to get the government to help them out. This was clearly brought out with beef. In 1973, during the year of the "beef shortage," cattle raisers were making extraordinary profits. In 1974, however, the market-clearing price of beef was so low that cattle raisers were slaughtering (and burying) calves, demanding a cessation of beef imports, and getting the government to increase its purchases of beef (i.e., attempting to shift the supply curve to the left and the demand curve to the right).

The government did, in fact, agree to purchase $100 million worth of "surplus" beef in that year. Many consumer groups complained that consumers were losing out to those in the cattle industry.

THE ECONOMICS OF
USURY LAWS

Moneylenders have long been the targets for endless vitupera-
tive attacks as bloodsucking leeches on society. The stigma has
been so great that dominant ethnic groups have historically
shunned the occupation, leaving it to minorities to serve the
borrowing needs of any given community, and consequently to
endure victimization, purges, and bloodlettings when scape-
goats were needed.

The history of usury laws is long indeed. It seems that they
can be traced back to the dawn of recorded history. Early
Babylonians did, in fact, permit credit but limited the rate of
interest. The Bible tells us that "Thou shall not lend upon
usury to thy brother, . . ." (Deut. 23:19–20). One of our earli-
est economists, Aristotle, considered moneylending to be ster-
ile. The breeding of money from money was considered unnat-
ural and was to be hated. In the Roman Republic interest
charges were explicitly forbidden but were permitted later
during the period of the Roman Empire.

When we come to the early Middle Ages, religious leaders
decided that interest on loans was indeed unjust. To Christians
of that period, humility and charity were the greatest virtues

—the value of earthly goods was played down. Legislation outside the Church responded to its influence, and in general interest charges and usury were regarded as synonymous.

By the fifteenth century, it was recognized that humans are not perfect. Martin Luther, along with other reformers, began to concede that creditors could not be explicitly prevented from charging interest.

In the eighteenth century, restrictions on the paying of interest were relaxed, but most nations did have legal maximum usury rates at so-called reasonable levels. In the United States, most usury laws were inherited from the British. They remained in force in this country even after they were repealed in Great Britain in 1854.

It would be convenient to think that the opposition to money-lending for *interesse* resulted from an ancient ignorance of economic principles. After all, why should individuals be willing to give up the use of their own money unless they were paid? Modern enlightenment on this topic has not, however, completely changed the picture. In fact, the persistence of legislation affecting the lending of money makes it clear that a widespread suspicion still lingers that the moneylender possesses some unique, shady, and monopolistic influence. Many states have enacted laws setting maximum rates of interest on loans to consumers, and the federal government has legislated the maximum interest rates for various uses of money. What are the consequences? To find out, we must examine the so-called money market.

The market for money is like any other market. The suppliers are individuals and institutions who are willing at a price (the interest rate) to forgo present command over current use of goods and services; and the higher the price, the more money they will lend. The demanders are many: consumers wanting to buy goods now and pay later, investors undertaking some enterprise, and governments. And, as with other goods and services, the lower the price, the more will be demanded. So far, so good! But the money market in fact is composed of a lot of submarkets—those for consumer loans, commercial credit, and real estate, to name a few. Each sub-market has its own institutions—consumer loan companies, finance companies, banks, savings and loan associations—which specialize in bringing particular classes of borrowers and lenders together. Moreover, the price of money is different in each market. For financing the purchase of an automobile, the effective interest rate may be 18 to 36 percent per year; yet a corporation may be able to borrow for 9 percent, and the federal government for 7 percent. These rates also fluctuate over time with overall changes in the supply and demand for loans.[1]

What concerns us, however, is an explanation of the variations in rates at any given moment in time. Several factors determine the differences, other things being equal. First is the length of the loan. The longer the time period involved, the less certain lenders can be about conditions at the time of repayment; consequently, they demand higher compensation. Second is the degree of risk. A lender who feels that a given loan is excessively risky will ask a high rate of interest. Finally, the cost of administering the loan must be considered. It frequently costs as much to handle a small loan as a large one; therefore, the "load" factor, or handling charge, is necessarily a much higher percentage of a small than a large loan. Since this is a charge added to the "pure" price, it implicitly shows up as a higher interest rate.

Each type of loan has its own characteristics. For example, automobile loans are more risky than most and impose a high handling cost. Corporate loans may be for a long or short period, and are subject to risk varying with the credit reputation of the company. Since they usually involve substantial amounts of money, the handling charges constitute a relatively small percentage of the total cost of such loans. The federal government issues short-term notes which are in effect riskless; because of the government's taxing power, they cannot be de-

---

[1] In addition, during periods of inflation these rates will go higher, reflecting the fact that suppliers are willing to loan money only at greater interest than before because when they are paid back the money will be worth less than it was when it was borrowed.

faulted. They also involve substantial sums and therefore small handling charges per dollar involved. The net result of these factors is a relatively low rate of interest.

The suppliers of loanable funds can reasonably be expected to shift their funds from one submarket to another depending on where they can obtain the highest rate of return, adjusted for time, risk, and handling charges. However, they must have access to information on all of these possible outlets for their money. Since a wide variety of agencies and news media dispenses this information at very low cost, the overall capital market tends to be very responsive to changes which affect the rates of return to various suppliers.

To return now to the question of usury laws: Suppose a state legislates a maximum interest rate of 12 percent on consumer loans. If this is higher than the generally prevailing interest rate, it has no effect. However, this is an unlikely assumption. Even in the absence of inflationary tendencies, the going rate on run-of-the-mill consumer transactions is normally higher than 12 percent. What, then, is the effect of the restriction? At the lower rate, buyers will demand more money than the finance companies are willing to supply at that return. Lenders will begin by introducing service charges to cover "handling costs" which formerly were incorporated in the interest rate. Then they will move to some sort of rationing of the funds available for loans. Logically, they will attempt to eliminate the riskier loans; and since empirically the risk of default on loans is inversely related to the income of the borrower, the refusal of loans to the lowest-income groups will offer the easiest course—that is, the least costly procedure in terms of acquiring information about potential borrowers. The predictable outcome, therefore, is that loans will be made only to the higher-income groups and the would-be borrower whose income is low will face a closed door.

We should investigate the allegations of those who support a ceiling on interest rates. The charges cover two areas: (a) that a monopolistic conspiracy exists among loan companies to maintain a high rate of interest; and (b) that the interest rate is too high because of legislation, presumably inspired by the loan companies, to restrict entry of new companies into the consumer-finance field.

No *a priori* judgment is possible on either contention without an examination of conditions in the consumer-loan market in each state. In any case, however, the solution to the problem of rates that are higher than the competitive level cannot be found in the fixing of an arbitrary ceiling, for the reason just described. Rather, the solution must lie in vigorous prosecution of any conspiracy or in the repeal of laws unduly restricting entry into the field.

We can take a number of real-world examples to find out the effects of usury laws on the allocation of credit across states. At the writing of this book, the state of Arkansas, for example, prohibited any lender from charging more than 10 percent simple interest per year on a loan. That state's Supreme Court has taken the position that a loan carries one basic charge— interest. It has not allowed lenders to get around the 10 percent ceiling by any of the various devices, such as adding finance charges, service or commitment fees, points, or other extras. Further, any lender found guilty of usury in Arkansas stands to lose the full value of the loan. In one case, for example, an auto dealer who sold a car under an installment plan that was later declared usurious could not recover interest principal or even the car itself.

If we want to see the effects of such a usury law in the state of Arkansas, we need go no further than to look at the border-straddling cities of Texarkana, where Arkansans and Texans live together separated only by a street. In Texas the usury laws are more lenient. On the Texas side of Texarkana there are eleven new car dealers but none on the Arkansas side. The Texas city boasts twenty-three used-car dealers to the Arkansas' three. On the Texas side, there are over twenty furniture and appliance dealers, while the Arkansas city has only six. Why does this happen? Simply because at the 10 percent rate of interest allowed by the state law, it is not worthwhile for businesspersons in Arkansas to lend for such purchases as cars and TVs.

This was not always a problem, particularly in the bygone era when we had no inflation; but today we have inflation and sometimes of the double-digit kind. When inflation is 10 percent a year and a bank is allowed to lend out money at 10 percent a year, what do you think the real return on that loan is? If a dollar is lent out for one year and there is a rate of inflation of 10 percent, the purchasing power or value of that dollar has fallen to 90 cents. If the bank can only charge 10 percent on that loan, it will get $1.10—barely enough to make up for the loss in purchasing power of the dollar loaned out. It has to loan out money at an interest rate higher than the rate of inflation in order to make a real rate of return that is above zero. It is not surprising that states that have very strict usury laws are suffering from a loss of business to other surrounding states that do not have strict usury laws.

Restrictions on economic variables always have consequences by which some gain and some lose. Economic analysis can help identify both the effects of the restrictions and the groups affected. Restrictions on interest rates lead to curtailment of the supply of loans, with lower-income groups being most adversely affected.

12

THE ECONOMICS OF
MEDICAL CARE

Today we face soaring medical costs, widespread fraud in payments for medical services and insistent demand for national health insurance. While historically we have had a "shortage" of doctors, now we are told that there may be too many in the near future. Let us see how this came about.

Expenditures for medical care in the United States increased from under $4,000,000,000 in 1929 to more than $140,000,000,000 in 1977. In 1940 per capita expenditures on health were $29 and by 1980 it is projected they may be over $800. Put another way the percentage of gross national product going for health expenditures was approximately 4 percent in 1929 and will be close to 10 percent in 1980. About 52 percent of this increase in expenditures on medical care is a result of price increases. Almost 10 percent is a result of population growth, but 38 percent is a result of increased use and improvements in quality.

A basic explanation for this last change has been that medical care is *income elastic*. That is, as the American population's income has risen since 1929 it has devoted a bigger percentage of that incremental income to medical care. A second reason is that the consumer pays less than the full cost of health services. Direct consumer payments represent only about 35 cents out of each dollar. The remainder comes from third parties, in particular private health insurance and government. Two major government programs, Medicare and Medicaid, have been particularly important. In 1975 the combined estimated cost of these two programs was more than twenty billion dollars. Indeed, in recent years, approximately 2/5 of the growth in health costs have been attributable to the growth in Medicare and Medicaid expenditures. So much for the history of the demands for medical care. Now let us look at the supply side.

When the American Medical Association (AMA) was founded in 1847, it adopted two basic policy positions: That doctors should be licensed, and that schools of medicine must be accredited. The first policy was quickly adopted by state legislatures but the second was not enacted until state medical schools recommended that a substantial number of schools be closed and standards for the remainder be raised. The state legislatures delegated the task of accrediting the medical schools to the AMA. Since one could not receive a license to practice without graduating from an accredited school, the result was the restriction of the supply of licensed doctors to graduates of these schools. Severe accrediting requirements led to a reduction in the number of medical schools from 162 in 1904 to 69 in 1920. The 1904 figure was not reached again until the mid-1950s. As a consequence, the number of doctors per 100,000 population dropped from 157 in 1900 to 148 in 1960. Since throughout this period the demand for medical services was growing but the supply was not increasing at a comparable rate, the price of doctors could be expected to rise, and it did. For the period 1939 to 1951 the mean income of physicians increased 218 percent, a substantially greater jump than occurred in any other profession. However, beginning in the 1960s, there was a reversal in this pattern, partly because doctors trained abroad came and practiced in the United States. Despite some opposition from the American Medical Association, the percentage of physicians trained abroad has increased until in 1973 it was 24 percent of all doctors practicing in the United States. As the AMA's grip over medical schools gradually declined, the number of doctors per 100,000 population has grown until in 1972 it had risen to 174 per 100,000.

That isn't the whole story. There has been equal rise in number of nurses per 100,000 population, and the development of a new group of paramedical hospital personnel. A great many of the aspects of medical care can be undertaken by someone with less training than a doctor, but with more medical training than nurses. A development of an intermediate group of paramedical services has filled this gap, and has contributed to the growth of medical personnel. Now with this background, let us turn and look at contemporary issues.

From the consumer's point of view, rapid price increases in the cost of physician's services may not be as obvious in the future. Medical schools are now graduating about 10,000 students per year, compared to the 7500 in 1965. By 1980, medical schools are projected to be graduating 15,000 M.D.'s per year. The licensing of foreign doctors adds another 3,000 per year; thus, the projection by 1980 is that we will have close to 450,000 M.D.'s in the United States. That means that physicians are growing at four times the population rate.

In economic terms, we are therefore witnessing a shift outward in the supply curve for physicians.[1] If the demand curve for medical services does not shift as rapidly, then the relative price of physicians will fall and we will expect that physicians' salaries will not be increasing as rapidly as they have in the past. There are indications that the demand curve for physicians and health services in general may shift as fast or even faster than the shift in the supply curve of physicians. We have already mentioned that the demand curve shifts out because health care is income elastic and we are a nation that experiences growths in income just about every year. However, there is another factor that we must consider—national health insurance.

[1] There are now more restrictions on licensing of foreign-trained M.D.'s; the supply curve may not be shifting out so rapidly.

By the time you read this book, some form of national health insurance may already be in effect. There have been over the years a large number of alternative national health insurance plans. The differences in these plans mainly concern the degree to which the individual participates in paying for medical expenses. At one extreme, the participant pays nothing; at the other extreme, the participant pays 100 percent of a certain minimum amount of expenses and, say, 20 percent of all medical expenses incurred over that cut-off point in any one year. Thus, a deductible as is common in most insurance policies, has been suggested for national health insurance. Let us focus for a moment on the effects of such a deductible.

With a national health insurance plan in which there is a zero deductible, that is, all medical payments are paid by the government, the direct price of medical care falls to zero for those who are eligible. Presumably, such eligibility would depend on one's annual income. Thus, at, say, $10,000 annual income, the family would not be eligible for the zero deductible. Consider then a family making less than that cut-off point who incurs medical expenses during the year. All of those expenses will be fully paid by the government. What will happen, therefore, to the quantity of medical care of the "small" nature demanded by such families? In the aggregate, we may predict that if the price elasticity of demand for medical care is not zero, the quantity demanded will increase, perhaps even greatly, by such families who face the zero deductible. What we are saying is that more of these families will seek medical care for minor problems, such as colds, sprained ankles, skin rashes, and the like. Why? Because the out-of-pocket costs for such medical consultation will fall to zero.

Thus, the imposition of a deductible on those families would mean that the quantity of medical care demanded by them would not increase as greatly in such a national health care plan. It is not surprising, therefore, that even staunch advocates of national health insurance strongly believe that a significant deductible must be included so as to discourage individuals from turning to physicians for every slight malady they suffer.

If a plan is put into effect which ignores the increased quantity of medical services demanded in the absence of a significant deductible, then projected costs to the government will greatly underestimate what actual costs will be. This is exactly what happened when Medicare was put into effect. It cost the government many billions of dollars more per year than ever anticipated because the cost estimates were based on the then-current quantity of medical services demanded by elderly people. That quantity increased dramatically when the relative price facing them for such services fell, in effect, to zero. Note, however, that physicians and the medical profession in general would benefit by having a national insurance plan that had a zero or low deductible. Medical professionals would be in greater demand.

The way in which national health insurance is financed is in a sense a red herring. Some proposals suggest that the employer pay all or part of the costs of national health insurance. Others suggest that the employer and the employee share it. And still others want the employer to pay part and general income tax revenues to pay the remainder. The point is that the total resources that are used in the national health insurance scheme are resources given up by society. It matters little from a resource allocation point of view how they are financed, provided that the financing is not attached to the use of the system. If the employer pays a fixed amount or the employee pays a fixed amount or the monies come out of general tax revenues, the fact remains that the user of the national health care system does not face a direct price each time he or she seeks health care. Individuals respond to the direct prices charged them for the use of resources. And in any type of national health insurance scheme, those who are healthy end up subsidizing those who are less healthy. There is virtually no way around this problem.

THE ECONOMICS OF
RISK AND
INSURANCE

You have just inherited $10,000, and you are trying to figure how best to invest it. Should you put it into stocks, bonds, a savings account, or perhaps a down payment on a house?

If you choose to invest in stocks, for example, which stock should you pick and how do you know that it is going to go up in value? In fact, every time you buy a stock, one or more other persons are selling it and betting that they can do better by putting their money in something else; that is, they are suggesting that there is a better buy. Anyone who has been involved in stocks over any length of time knows that the market has a very uncertain future. Well then, what about bonds? They are certainly much more secure. But even bondholders at times have found out that bonds can be risky, as was the case for holders of Penn Central bonds some years ago. Well then, a savings account is surely the answer. After all, it is backed by the federal government so that savings are insured up to $40,000 by the Federal Deposit Insurance Corporation. Well, let's say that your savings account is paying you 6 percent interest and along comes inflation at 10 percent. Thus you have a negative real interest rate (in terms of purchasing

power). There surely must be a better way. It certainly has
been true that land and housing investments have often been
profitable, but you put a down payment on a house and shortly
thereafter the local airport authority changes the runways so
the approach pattern of jets is now over your home. There goes
that profitable investment.

In short, there is no guarantee of a road to the promised
land. We all face the vagaries of chance. Fire can strike our
houses. Robbery can deprive us of valuable possessions, and
so on. Nor is this uncertainty confined to investments. We all
take chances every day in our lives in a world of uncertainty.
An investment decision is in some respects similar to choosing
a wife or a husband. We cannot predict with confidence how
it is going to turn out. That does not mean that we cannot alter
the amount of risk that we take. In fact, every day in life people choose among more or less risky paths of activity. Thus we
can spend a lifetime in a federal bureaucratic job in which
there is much less risk of being terminated or fired but in
which the opportunities for large income are less. Alterna-
tively, we can go for broke by putting all of our savings in the
development of some new product in the one-in-a-hundred
chance that we will get a high return. But then there is always
the 99 percent chance that we will lose.

We cannot eliminate risk altogether, but we can systemati-
cally reduce it through insurance, and the prevalence of insurance in almost every activity in life is testimonial to our widespread desire to reduce or spread risks in a more uniform
manner. In order for insurance to succeed, we must have a
large enough number covered by it and also we must be able
to actuarily determine the risk by individuals within that
group. For example, there is no way to predict whose house is
going to burn down, but if enough houses are insured and we
have statistics on fires in dwellings, we can safely predict that
a certain number of houses will burn every year, and therefore
determine an insurance rate on houses. Insurance companies
estimate the frequency of loss-causing events for specific
groups and locations. When such estimates are obtained, insur-

ance premiums can be calculated. The insurance company takes into account the frequency of particular events, such as house fires, and also the loss payments that must be made to compensate the persons or businesses that suffer the losses. Obviously, for the insurance company to make a profit, it must have good data for its estimate. It must charge higher insurance premiums when losses occur more frequently and also for higher-value losses.

We can illustrate this with automobile insurance. Automobile insurance companies are competitive with each other, and therefore each firm strives to find ways to lower the price of their particular insurance. Therefore, companies have continually searched the data on specific groups of people and cars to find out where the probability of accidents was lowest. Hence we find that compact cars were insured for a smaller premium because data are shown insurance companies that these types of vehicles are involved in less costly accidents. Young people who have passed the driver training course pay less for insurance because data have shown that they are also involved in fewer accidents.

Clearly, we can reduce the risks in life by insurance, but we cannot do away with them completely. The world of uncertainty still exists.

4

THE ECONOMICS OF SAVING OUR CITIES

In 1975 the largest city in the United States almost went under. New York teetered on the verge of bankruptcy for many months. Some people blamed the past extravagances of city politicians. After all, they had allowed public servants to earn some of the highest salaries in the nation and welfare recipients to obtain some of the highest benefits around. Others blamed the federal government. After all, they maintained, New York was the financial and business capital of the country and, therefore, bestowed benefits on everyone, but did not receive a sufficient amount of federal aid to compensate for the costs incurred. Also it was noted that many welfare recipients had moved in from many other states which had lower aid levels; thus New York, in addition to aiding its own indigents, was being asked to help out the rest of the nation's poor.

Whatever the cause of New York City's financial distress was, for many months the federal government, that is, the president and Congress, repeatedly insisted that New York City was going to have to stew in its own juice. However, a compromise was finally reached in which the federal government loaned some money to the city. It is remarkable that at that time

President Ford indicated that the taxpayers throughout the United States would not in effect be paying for helping New Yorkers out. He, of course, was committing a basic economic fallacy in saying that. The funds committed to help New York City out, even if repaid in the future, could have been used somewhere else. Hence, the opportunity cost of the $2.5 billion loaned to the city of New York was really the cost to American taxpayers in general. There is no such thing as a free loan even if the federal government is giving it to a city government.

We note that the federal government's "bail-out" plan required that it have first claim on city revenues to pay off that loan. This may seem like shrewd bargaining but our interest in such a provision goes far beyond. That provision was enacted without any of the then-current creditors of New York being asked for their permission, even though they were also owed large sums of money by the city.

Herein lies a major problem that the New York City financial fiasco serves to highlight. Cities all around the country often desire to make capital improvements such as in public housing, roads, and the like. Also, there are periods when cities temporarily have insufficient revenues to pay for all previously contracted expenses. In such cases, the city goes to the commercial bond market in order to borrow money from the private sector. It will sell municipal bonds. It is the ability of cities to raise capital in this manner which often allows them to do many of the things that the voters have agreed the city should undertake. But the city's ability to sell bonds to people in the private sector depends in large part on the certainty that the bondholders will be repaid. How much certainty would you have that New York City was going to pay you back if the city fathers agreed that the federal government was to have first claim on city revenues to pay back the loan to Washington? Certainly less than if you as a previous bondholder had *first* claim.

This whole issue can be thought of in terms of the actual rights that you have in something that you own. Let's say you purchased a bond ten years ago from the city of New York. In that bond was a provision (called a covenant) which said that you had the right to the tax revenues of the city in the event that the city went bankrupt. This is a common provision in municipal bonds; as a bondholder you would be willing to pay more for such a bond than you would for one which did not give you such a right. The Local Finance Law in New York explains that such bonds ". . . are issued in anticipation of the receipt of such revenues as State aid for education, local non-property taxes, etc. When these revenues are received, they must be used only for the payment of these notes [bonds] as they become due."

You can be certain that if you had purchased one of those bonds ten years ago and were holding it in June 1975, you would have been surprised and, indeed, enraged. In that month, the New York State Legislature established the Municipal Assistance Corporation ("Big Mac"). The law that established "Big Mac" stated that the above-mentioned revenues would not go first to you as a bondholder, but rather would be used first to pay for what the state felt were essential services in New York City. It is not difficult now to understand why the value of that bond you might have been holding would have fallen drastically. You had just lost a property right, as it were, in the future stream of revenues collected by the city. You might have been compensated for this loss of a property right but in the case of New York, no one was compensated. In fact, for a five-month period, the city stopped paying interest on $1.6 million of its bonds and offered instead "Big Mac" bonds in exchange. But since those bonds were neither an enforceable obligation nor a debt of either New York State or New York City, it would seem that the unfortunate holders of New York City bonds were not getting anything.

If what happened in New York City was merely an isolated case, then presumably other cities in the future will not have any increased difficulty in raising money by selling bonds; however, we note that there are an increasing number of cases where well-established legal property rights expressed in bond contracts are being abrogated by various government bodies.

In 1975 the New York and New Jersey State Legislatures repealed a Port Authority law relating to all Port Authority bonds issued since 1962. That particular covenant prevented the Port Authority from financing any deficit-ridden mass transit systems. The legislature, however, repealed the law and allowed the Authority to go ahead and do what it was formerly prevented from doing. Then-current Port Authority bondholders could not be certain about their getting paid interest and principal. The market price of those bonds fell significantly as soon as it was known that the legislature was going to repeal the covenant. Note again that here no compensation was made to the bondholders who suffered these windfall losses.

We could go on and on with similar cases of alterations in the property rights an individual thought he or she had. During the earlier part of this decade, bondholders in the Penn Central Railroad found that the government wiped out their contractual rights as bondholders without one cent in compensation. Such activity on the part of governments will make it increasingly difficult for a governmental body and firms in regulated industries to raise what is called debt capital, that is, to borrow money. The market value of a piece of paper that is called a bond depends on the certainty that the owner of that piece of paper has a claim in the future stream of income. It really doesn't matter what the bond says if the owner faces the possibility of a government simply destroying some contractual aspect of the bond. The property right of that bondholder has been seriously attenuated in such a situation. The market value of the bond will fall. Hence, the only way that city governments will be able to finance spending by borrowing from the private sector will be by offering ever higher interest rates in order to compensate the purchaser of their bonds for the increased riskiness. Thus, the way in which New York City and the federal government handled the New York City crisis may have straightened things out in the short run, but might cause even more serious problems in the long run if private investors consider municipal bond markets to be an unsafe investment.

THE ECONOMICS OF JURIES

In all criminal prosecutions, the accused shall enjoy the right to a speedy and public trial, by an Impartial Jury of the state and district wherein the crime shall have been committed, which district shall have been previously ascertained by law, and to be informed of the nature and cause of the accusation: . . .

So reads the Sixth Amendment of the United States Constitution. We all have the right to trail by a jury, a jury presumably of our peers. In 1976, numerous trials by jury took place involving thousands of "impartial" jurors who spent a total of 16.4 million man-days pondering the different cases before them. Our jury system involves a tremendous amount of human resources each year. We have become accustomed to such a system and also to the way in which jurors are selected in this country. Surprisingly, however, the methods used for jury selection are not radically different from those that were used when we had the military draft. Military conscription was for a number of years under widespread attack and finally it was, for all practical purposes, eliminated.

In any conscription system, the chosen participants rarely have much choice about whether or not to undertake the new task assigned to them. When we had the military draft, we did allow some individuals to "escape" the draft. During the Civil War, for example, men in the North who were conscripted were allowed to "buy" someone else to go in their stead. Therefore, even though the method of conscription was arbitrary, the final determination of who would go to war was more flexible. For example, a lawyer who found himself conscripted had the option of paying someone else to replace him. As long as the price he paid was lower than the amount he could earn by remaining at work, both parties benefited financially from the arrangement. Since many workers did not earn as much as a lawyer could (that is, their opportunity costs were lower), it was not hard to find a replacement at a mutually agreeable price. Since a person's contribution to the economy can be roughly indicated by his or her salary, it can be said in economists' terminology that an *efficient*[1] *allocation of resources* resulted since men worked (or fought) where their services were of most value.

Let's detour for a moment into a fuller discussion of this question of allocation of resources. Inefficiency exists whenever labor and machines are being used in such a manner that their full potential to the output of the economy is not being realized. A change from an inefficient to an efficient allocation therefore results, by definition, in an increase in output. This does not mean that everyone will be better off. All changes in our economy carry certain costs, and those who incur these costs are worse off. But in theory the increase in output allows those who bear the costs of the change to be fully compensated, assuming, of course, that some institutional mechanism exists by means of which the compensating "side payment" can be carried out.

In later years of the military draft, students were deferred,

[1] The term "efficient" as used in economics does not have any connotation of "good," "desirable," or "best," but merely refers to the most productive source of available resources.

special hardship cases were deferred, and so on. So, it was not strictly correct to say that everyone had to serve.

It is also not strictly correct to say that everyone must, if called, serve on a jury. There are many acceptable excuses that a prospective juror can offer to get out of serving.

Nonetheless, we do have hundreds of thousands of individuals serving on juries, whether voluntarily or not, and being paid a wage rate which is below that person's opportunity cost, that is, which is below that person's foregone earnings in the job that that person has. The cost to society of any resource is that resource's social opportunity cost. If we approximate social opportunity cost by wages earned, then we see that the social cost of our jury system far exceeds the actual payment in jury fees to those who serve in deciding the fate of the accused. Economist Donald L. Martin has made some tentative estimates of the difference between the social cost of juries and the actual payment of jury fees. His data for 1962 show that the social cost was $233 million compared to the total jury fees of $89 million. Estimates for 1976 are $487 million and $191 million respectively. Those data were based on a relatively random selection of jurors from a large list of, say, voter registrations or telephone directories. However, the cost would have been significantly higher had the so-called keyman system been used. In that system, certain "pillars" of the community (keymen) are asked to make up a list of prospective jurors. Presumably, keymen would select individuals from occupations with higher opportunity costs, that is, from higher-paying jobs. Professor Martin's estimate for 1962 was that such a system would cost almost $50 million more.

Actually, the cost of the current jury system is even higher than we have indicated. Since individuals are in general paid less for serving on juries than for staying on their jobs, they will seek to avoid being forced to serve on a jury; thus, more people must be called than are served and, hence, administrative costs will be higher as well as the individual cost incurred to avoid jury conscription.

Another inefficiency cost that arises has to do with the way in which the judicial system uses jurors as compared to other inputs in the legal process, such as judges. If the relative price of jurors facing the judicial system is below its social opportunity cost, then jurors will be used "excessively." That is to say, there will be too much idleness or waiting by jurors. On the other hand, there will be too little idleness on the part of judges, since presumably they are "correctly" priced because they voluntarily remain on the job at the stated salary.

What alternative system might we use as a substitute for the current one? Professor Martin suggests the volunteer option. Just as we have now switched to a volunteer army, we could presumably switch to a volunteer jury system. When we say voluntary, we mean that the judicial system would have to pay a wage rate to jurors sufficient to induce them to voluntarily leave their work for the required number of days of the trial and decision-making period. We might predict that if we went to an all-volunteer system of jurors, that we would reduce some of the economic inefficiency due to (1) the use of, on occasion, relatively high opportunity-cost jurors, and (2) the excessive use of jurors compared to other inputs into the judicial system.

Some may argue that a volunteer system would be too expensive, the taxpayers would not be willing to pay the higher bill. However, this is beside the point; taxpayers as a whole, that is, all of society, are paying the social opportunity cost of the jury system whether or not it is fully explicit. Currently, only about forty percent of the costs of jurors is paid for by taxpayers, but the other sixty percent is paid nonetheless in terms of the social opportunity cost that goes into the jury system. As in many situations, the explicit payment for a resource does not fully measure the cost to society.

There is also another potential problem with an all-volunteer jury system. Such a system would, in all likelihood, *ex*-clude high-income individuals. Thus, it would not represent much of a cross-section of the population nor could we be assured that accused individuals would be tried by a jury of their "peers." Presumably, advocates of a volunteer jury system must come up with a way to cope with this bias in such a selection process.

16

THE ECONOMICS OF
PROFESSIONAL SPORTS

More than a decade ago, the Washington Redskins drafted
star defensive back Jim (Yazoo) Smith. His record at the University of Oregon was impressive; and as a rookie, he was good
enough to crack the starting lineup for the Redskins. Unfortunately, in the final game of the season Smith suffered a
severe neck injury that permanently ended his career. Things
didn't end there, however.

In September 1976, U.S. Judge William B. Bryant awarded
Jim Smith $276,000 in damages—not because of his physical
injuries, but because he suffered financial losses. Smith had
sued the National Football League for violation of antitrust
laws. He contended that the League's draft system (which
we will describe in more detail below) had restricted his
bargaining power with the Redskins. He further contended
that the negotiations were so lopsided that he was prevented
from obtaining a contract that would have given him financial
security when and if he suffered any disabling injury.

This was not the first lawsuit that had been brought against
the National Football League Association. A few years earlier,
U.S. District Court Judge William T. Sweigert ruled in favor

of football player Joe Kapp and against the National Football League. Judge Sweigert ruled that the standard player contract was illegal in that it bound a player to one team.

The NFL suffered another legal setback in 1975 when U.S. Judge Earl Larson declared the so-called Rozelle Rule invalid. Pete Rozelle has been the Commissioner of the National Football League for a number of years. The system worked as follows: A player would leave his team after his contract had expired. He would go to a new team. Then, Commissioner Rozelle could take players or draft choices away from that new team and give them to the team that lost the player.

Football has not been the only professional sport that has seen lawsuits brought by players against team owners. For example, baseball player Curt Flood brought an antitrust action against professional baseball league owners. He was specifically attacking the so-called reserve clause in the standard baseball players' contracts. When the case reached the Supreme Court in 1972, Flood lost, even though Justice Harry A. Blackman said that he realized that the clause was "an aberration."

Why would professional players bring antitrust suits against the leagues in which they play? How can a standard player contract bind the player to the team? What is the reserve clause? These are some of the issues that we will treat in the following few pages.

The reserve clause binds a player to work exclusively for the team which holds his contract; the player can be traded to another team without his permission. If he does not like his salary or working conditions, his only option is to quit the game altogether.

To gain perspective, let us look first at a labor market which has no reserve clause: the market for gardeners. Most gardeners charge what they think is the "going" price for their services. If one charges considerably less than this price, some potential additional customers will eventually find out. He will then find himself with many new requests for his services. If he is not willing to put extra hours into gardening, he will have to decide on one, or a combination, of the following courses:

(a) he can lower the quality of his service so that each job requires less time, and he can squeeze in more customers; (b) he can refuse the additional work; (c) he can raise his prices so that certain customers, present or potential, will not be interested in obtaining his services. Obviously the first choice is equivalent to the third one, since a change in quality at the same price exerts the same economic effect as a change in price for the same quality.

On the other hand, if a gardener who does not have enough work wishes to attract more customers, he is free to lower his price or raise the quality of his services. That is, gardeners can compete among themselves to maximize their own individual incomes. To be sure, not all gardeners do this.

Now let's assume that a particular gardener gains a reputation for doing exceptionally good work. If he already has a full schedule, a potential customer will have to offer some incentive to gain his services on a regular basis. An adequate incentive might persuade the gardener to do one of the following: (a) work more intensively, (b) work longer hours and take fewer holidays, (c) drop one of his former customers.

The usual form of inducement is an offer of higher wages, although the award might be nonmonetary. In any case, by employing such tactics people desiring to obtain gardeners' services are competing among themselves. Although not all homeowners take the trouble to find out which gardener in the neighborhood gives the best service at the lowest price, some do.

We have just described the workings of a competitive market in gardening. The gardeners are free to vary the price, quantity, and quality of the service they sell. Homeowners are free to vary the price (wage) they offer, and the quantity and quality of service they demand. Theoretically, gardeners end up getting a wage that just equals the value of their services (i.e., they are paid the value of their marginal product). Buyers of gardeners' services end up just paying for the opportunity cost of these services, no more, no less (i.e., they must pay the value of the gardeners' marginal product).

What would happen if all homeowners in the country got together and decided to institute a "gardening reserve clause"? The reserve clause would require that each individual gardener work for only one homeowner (or, more realistically in this case, for one group of owners). The gardener could not work anywhere else unless the owner of the contract with the reserve clause decided that he, the owner, wanted to sell or trade the contract. Notice that one crucial aspect of the previously described competitive market has been eliminated: Gardeners cannot seek out the most advantageous job opportunities or compete for business, because only the homeowners can initiate a move. It is surely apparent that such restraint would prevent gardeners from seeking employment that would maximize their income and that it could leave them worse off than they were under free and competitive conditions.

They not only could but most certainly *would* be worse off if all homeowners then got together to form a cartel with the express agreement that they would not compete among themselves for gardeners' contracts. Competition in the gardening market would be stifled on both sides: among the sellers of gardening services and among the buyers of those services.[1]

What is pure hypothesis in our example has become stern reality in the world of baseball. Within the major leagues, teams have made up an interlocking set of agreements among themselves which yields a very special players' contract. Since the terms include an agreement not to tamper with a player "reserved" by any team, the contracting club in effect holds a unilateral option on the player's services for the following year. Once the player signs, he must accept all the agreements made between teams; therefore, his only course is to attempt to get the highest salary possible from his particular team with no help from other competing teams. His choice is simple: to

---

[1] Of course it is hard to imagine a cartel of so many people actually working. The incentive to cheat would be too great, the problem of inducing new homeowners to join would be large, and the cost of enforcement of the agreement would be tremendous.

accept the offered salary or not to play baseball—at least not
with any U.S. major league team.

The reserve clause allows a baseball team to restrain the
workings of the job market for baseball players. Therefore, a
monopoly element enters into baseball hirings.[2] Baseball teams
contend that the reserve clause is essential to the game because
it allows for an even distribution of good players among all
teams. It is asserted that without the reserve rules richer clubs
would bid away all the best talent. Games would be lopsided,
and bored spectators would quit buying tickets.

Although plausible at first glance, this argument loses validity when it is realized that any industry could make a similar
statement. In practice rich firms do not buy up all the best
workers and thus make the manufacturing "game" lopsided.
Firms and baseball clubs can always borrow money to invest
in good workers and good players if the potential payoff from
doing so is high enough. Obviously, if only one good (rich)
team existed, the payoff from building a competing good team
would be high enough to allow a club to borrow money (or
sell additional stock) in order to do so.

Moreover, the value of players depends on gate receipts.
How large would ticket sales be with only one good team?
Few people would want to see a slaughter at every game involving the best, richest team. Therefore, it behooves good
teams to make sure that there are other good teams to play
with in order to generate suspense, excitement, and the resulting higher gate receipts.

The Sherman Antitrust Act specifically forbids action in restraint of trade, but the Supreme Court ruled in 1922 that
owners of baseball teams were exempt from such federal legislation; the ruling was upheld in 1953 and in 1972. But the reserve clause is an attempt to restrict competition among teams
for players. Hence, players are making less money now than
they would without the reserve clause.

It might appear that competition among teams to sign new-
comers could eliminate some of the exploitation of players. For

[2] The technically correct term is *monopsony*—one buyer.

a while "side payments" to new players did serve this end, but now a draft system has been inaugurated under which no such payments are allowed.

The impact of the reserve clause on players' salaries was, for quite some time, augmented by the effects of a compact between the National and American leagues *not* to compete for each other's players. Such an arrangement obviously would suggest the potential for a third league to bid the best players away from the other two by offering higher salaries. No third U.S. league could have succeeded, however, because players who might have signed with it would be forever barred from the American and the National leagues. Apparently not enough players were willing to take this chance, and no other major league appeared.

In an attempt to counter the monopoly power of the baseball team owners, a union has been formed consisting of baseball players. That union has been successful both directly in raising players' salaries and indirectly by improved pension plans. The union has also vigorously fought the reserve clause and other restrictive labor arrangements in professional baseball.

Professional football is almost the image of professional baseball. There was only one league, the NFL, from 1919 until 1960, when the AFL appeared. Players' salaries promptly shot upward manyfold.

When the NFL ruled the scene, teams could "draft" players and that was it. No competition by larger salary offers was allowed. The players were thus prevented from maximizing their incomes by a collusive agreement among NFL team owners. And there was no competing league to bid players away.

The NFL draft system started in 1936; it prohibits a college player from negotiating with any professional team other than the one that drafted him. Generally, the worst teams in the league get the first draft choices, presumably to give them a better chance in the forthcoming season. At the beginning of this chapter we talked about the suit won by Jim (Yazoo) Smith. When the judge in that case, William Bryant, struck down the NFL's annual draft of college players, he commented that "this outright, undisguised refusal to deal constitutes a group boycott in its classic and most pernicious form, a device which has long been condemned as per se violation of the antitrust laws." Bryant further added that the draft procedure was "absolutely the most restrictive one imaginable." He suggested that the NFL could change things a bit to satisfy the court. For example, the judge thought that three teams might be allowed to choose one player and then bid for that player's services. This, of course, would improve the bargaining position of the players.[3]

In 1966, after six years of "competition," the AFL and NFL agreed to merge. Congress approved the move as a rider to a public housing bill![4] This merger has affected the freedom of players. Although the terms state that after playing out his contract's one-year option the player may sign with any other team, that team has to compensate the one he left. This may be, of course, discouraging to the second team. The player can also attempt to arrange a trade through the offices of the Football Commissioner, but the results to date have not been very favorable to the players involved. The AFL–NFL merger, by precluding the need to compete for players, has obviously held the salaries of players lower than they would have been under freely competitive conditions.

The lack of competition in professional football could not last forever, however. The World Football League started to change the scene a few years ago. As a competing league, it sought to obtain players by offering what they wanted—higher salaries. Even though the World Football League folded because it had financial problems, the implications for our theory are borne out. When competition started in professional football, players' salaries started to skyrocket.

---

[3] Note that if no reserve clause existed, the draft system would not work because it would not allocate property rights; that is, without the reserve clause the team owners do not obtain the property rights in the players' contracts.

[4] This, in spite of a 1967 court ruling that football was subject to antitrust laws.

Professional hockey saw the same thing happen when the World Hockey Association came in to challenge the ever-powerful National Hockey League. Again, as we would expect, professional players' salaries in hockey skyrocketed when a competing league came in.

The situations described above do not necessarily indicate that team owners in professional sports actually planned along the lines of our analysis. Yet they need not have done so for our thesis to prove valid. We have provided a theory of collusive behavior with some obvious implications about players' salaries. The validity of the implications is borne out by the facts.

The times are changing in professional sports. The courts no longer appear to accept the sports business as being exempt from antitrust laws. Reserve clauses are fading into the background, as well as restrictive draft systems. Professional football, basketball, baseball, hockey, tennis, and soccer may, in the future, see team owners' monopsony power reduced substantially.

THE ECONOMICS OF
THE AUTOMOBILE

When historians look back on the twentieth century, they will probably label it the era of the automobile. No other single technological innovation during this century has caused a more fundamental change in people's pattern of living than the automobile. It has become a necessity, so much so indeed that there are more than half as many automobiles as people in America. When we take into account the number of eligible drivers, the ratio is more than one to one. As of this writing, we are still groping for ways to deal with the automobile. While it is a necessity, it is also a major cause of pollution, congestion, and, to many Americans, simple ugliness in the American landscape. Let's take a look at some of the costs to society of the American automobile before we see how we might deal with it. First we must distinguish costs to the individual car owner and user from costs borne by society as a whole.

When there is a divergence between these *private costs* and *social costs*, we say that an *externality* exists. Costs external to the private decision-maker are not included in his calculations. Thus an externality occurs because of the inability of all concerned to arrange a contractual agreement that would eliminate or at least reduce the problem. People adversely affected by your automobile exhaust cannot easily contract with you to eliminate the problem. So you go driving about without considering the social cost.

The automobile owner's private costs are his monthly loan payments, operating costs, and annual license fees. Included in operating costs are insurance and federal and state taxes on gasoline. Yet, each automobile owner imposes costs on society which greatly exceed his private costs. Let's see what the true social costs are.

Although recent federal and state laws have reduced the amount of air pollution caused by the automobile, it still accounts for approximately half of the air pollution we breathe.

Every time a driver enters a crowded freeway he contributes to the congestion, causing other drivers to arrive at their destinations just a little later. At rush hours everyone tries to use the freeways at the same time, with the result that no one goes anywhere. Each driver is therefore imposing a cost on every other driver. And what does our one motorist contribute to this nightmare? His contribution is the sum of the marginal costs in extra time imposed on all other drivers by his presence. If we value each driver's time as equal more or less to his wage rate (opportunity cost), then the social cost any one driver levies with respect to congestion is considerable.

As he drives down the road, a driver is also contributing to the noise that envelops the highway, and he is thus piling up more social costs. What would be the value of noise abatement, and what is the marginal contribution of each driver to the total of noise? Like so many problems involving social versus private costs, these are difficult questions. Perhaps values can be assigned only by determining how much the populace would be willing to pay to avoid this form of pollution.

"Visual pollution" is another social cost imposed by America's automobiling populace. The eye is offended by abandoned cars littering the roadsides, by junkyards of crumpled vehicles, and only slightly less by the 230,000 gas stations that stand shoulder to shoulder across the national landscape.

The real problem with these externalities is to find a valid measure of the social cost in each case and to discover an effective way to assess each driver according to his just share. This is not an impossible task. We are gradually discovering ways of isolating and imposing, if not the total social cost, at least enough of it to encourage the originator of the externality to alter his behavior.

Suppose, for example, that the goal is to eliminate the externalities caused by congestion in city streets. For a tollway, it is easy to impose charges that take account of all costs because the exits and entrances are relatively few. But how could city streets be metered effectively? A technological solution was suggested some years back by Professor William Vickrey, but it met with little success. He proposed that TV cameras be installed at those intersections where heaviest congestion occurred. It would then be possible to record the license numbers of all cars using these intersections at rush hours and to store the information in a computer. At the end of each month, motorists would be sent a bill for all the times they drove in the metered intersection.[1] To be sure, some motorists would avoid areas where metering devices were installed, but this would be all to the good. Motorists would then be driving in uncongested parts of the city or finding an alternative means of transportation.

When congestion occurs, many drivers are prevented from entering the city. These "losers" are not, at present, compensated in any way by those motorists who cause the congestion. What's more, motorists cannot be paid *not* to use the streets so as to reduce congestion.

The reader can perhaps see now that the problems created

---

[1] Another alternative suggested by Vickrey was the use of the Oxford electronic metering device, triggered by radio signals, since each passing car would emit a unique signal. Either procedure, however, raises the critical problem of invasion of privacy, since data stored in the computer could conceivably be released to other agencies.

by automobile drivers are in principle solvable if we can impose an increasing share of the social cost of the automobile on its owner. Motorists will then have an incentive to pressure producers to devise cars that are quieter and free of pollutants. If we can measure the pollution emitted by an engine and the noise a car generates, ways can be found to impose an appropriate tax on each owner. If tolls are levied on major access roads and varied according to rush hours, traffic congestion and peak-load problems can be reduced. If penalties are imposed for abandoned cars or rewards paid for turning them in, and if suitable penalties are laid on junkyards for pollution, the landscape will be improved.

One predictable obstacle to all such innovation is the political furor of the American motorist. His devotion to his own, private mode of transportation is well documented and is pointed up by the dilemma of urban mass-transit systems. From the New York subway to the Seattle bus system, these have one thing in common: They lose money.

One of the most dramatic cases in point of this decade is the San Francisco Bay area rapid transit system, or BART. BART was going to reduce traffic congestion, energy use, and air pollution. However, within just a few years after its belated beginning, transportation experts were starting to consider the whole idea a colossal mistake. Only one-half the number of daily riders are using the system than had been projected. The single rush hour ride on BART costs the rider more than twice as much as the trip by bus and 80 percent more than the trip in a small car, including parking. Barely one-third of BART's costs are covered by fare revenues. The rest is made up through property and sales taxes. Some of the profferred reasons for BART's dismal failure is that it simply is inconvenient. The stations are widely spaced so that the trains can run at high speed; thus, most commuters must take a bus or a car to the nearest station. Other examples of new modernistic mass transit systems would demonstrate the same point.

Nothing illustrates the dilemma of the automobile more clearly than the furor over gasoline prices since the 1973 Yom

Kippur War. In the face of the Arab boycott and the consequent sharp rise in gasoline prices (not to mention heating oil), politicians have pondered what to do. On the face of it, it should seem very simple. Here was a heaven-sent opportunity to reduce America's dependence on the automobile, either by letting the price rise so high that people would shift to other modes of transportation (or, at the very least, pool their transportation) or by rationing and simply cutting down on the amount of gasoline available. Either way would significantly reduce the social costs of pollution and congestion. But anyone would have thought that this heaven-sent opportunity was just the reverse as politicians wrung their hands and understandably so. Their constituents faced with this new dilemma were in no mood to do away with their faithful automobiles, and any politician who came out forthrightly against the automobile was in danger of becoming unemployed. It is not hard to see why. Whether the price of gasoline was dramatically increased or rationing imposed, it suddenly and seriously affected the way of life of a large number of people whose dependence on the automobile was deep and abiding. No matter which "solution" was tried, a large number of constituents and voters were going to be hurt. Since 1973 we have learned to live with higher gasoline prices and the American's love affair with the automobile continues unabated. The social costs are still with us—the problem unsolved.

8

THE ECONOMICS OF
TAXIS
AND
JITNEYS

The fact that you probably never heard of the word "jitney" says something about the problem we wish to pose in this issue. Jitneys, to all intents and purposes, disappeared from the urban American scene sometime ago as we shall see. But jitneys and taxis form a major basis of the transportation in urban areas at various times, past or present. For our purposes they illustrate a major dilemma of the transportation scene, namely, the use of political policies and regulatory devices in municipalities to restrict or eliminate certain kinds of competition with consequences for the overall efficiency of transportation on the American scene. Jitneys and taxis, therefore, are only symptomatic of the widespread dilemmas posed by regulation and restrictions on competition in transportation.

The dictionary defines a jitney as a "bus or car, especially one traveling a regular route, that carries passengers for a small fare, originally five cents." Believe it or not, there are a few places, even in the United States, where jitneys still exist, such as along Chicago's King Drive, San Francisco's Mission Street, and Atlantic City's Pacific Avenue. The jitney, however, is a common form of transportation in many foreign cities, such as along the Paseo de la Reforma in Mexico City, where they are called *peseros*. The principle of a jitney is simple. A vehicle, usually a normal-sized sedan but sometimes a small minibus, travels along a usually fixed route, taking on customers anywhere along that route until the vehicle is filled and dropping those customers off wherever they designate along that fixed route. In a modified situation, the jitney will (for an additional fee, of course) take a customer off the route but within a maximum range, only to return to the point of deviation for continuance along that same route. The distinguishing feature between a jitney and a regular taxi is that the latter cannot generally take on more than one paying set of customers and does not follow a fixed route. (As we shall see below, these restrictions are usually imposed by law, not by the taxi drivers themselves.)

Jitneys appeared on the American transportation scene prior to our entry into World War I. When jitneys first came on the scene, they offered advantages over the then prevalent mode of public transportation—electric street railways—namely, in the form of a higher average speed. That speed of 15 miles an hour was still twice as fast as streetcar speeds. Jitneys also had a greater flexibility in where they could depose a customer as compared with the absolutely fixed route of street railways.

The advantages of jitneys were sufficient at the prices charged to have them pose a serious competitive threat to the electric railway systems throughout the United States. In fact the *Electric Railway Journal* started referring to jitneys as "a menace," the "Frankenstein of transportation," and various other epithets. Competition by a competing mode of transportation would certainly mean an erosion in the profits of railway systems in municipalities. A general rule of thumb is: If when faced with competition you cannot compete on an economic basis, try the political arena. That is exactly what the railways did: They sought protection from governments of municipalities in which they were located. In spite of scattered newspaper support for projitney political policies, in spite of attempts by jitney association lobbyists, and in spite of the obvious anticompetitive implications of antijitney legislation, the restrictive legislation was passed throughout the United States.

At first the legislation required jitney operators to obtain licenses to use public streets as a place of business. This restriction drastically reduced the ease of entering this business, particularly given that the municipalities made it lengthy and costly to attempt to obtain such a permit or license. In some cities a license or franchise had to be submitted to voters! Additional costs were imposed, such as the requirement that relatively large liability bonds be purchased in order to protect the consumer of jitney services if a wrong was committed against him by a jitney operator. In some cases the total cost of licensing fees plus bonding requirements amounted to up to 50 percent of a jitney driver's annual earnings. This is the equivalent of a tax on drivers of that amount. In a highly competitive industry, where the individual participants were not making excessive profits, such a tax could only lead to one result—the elimination of a significant fraction of the industry's participants.

Further restrictions were added that basically eliminated the jitney as a form of public transportation in the United States. These included, among others, a requirement that any jitney had to be operated a minimum number of hours, that minimum usually exceeding the average number of hours that jitneys were usually run; the fixing of routes and schedules, thus eliminating the flexibility that jitneys offered; and the exclusion of jitneys from high-density downtown areas and specifically from trolley routes, thus eliminating the most advantageous working locations for the jitney drivers.[1] According to one student of jitney history, L. R. Nash,[2] within 18 months after the first appearance of jitneys in Los Angeles, antijitney (i.e., protrolley) regulatory ordinances had been passed in 125

[1] In 1974 the Los Angeles City Council removed its prohibition on jitney service. However, a proposed ordinance was soon put forth allowing the municipal bus system to restrict jitneys from operating along major bus routes. The city bus system successfully squashed plans to allow jitneys along heavily travelled routes. (History repeats itself.)

[2] L. R. Nash, "History and Economics of the Jitney," 18 *Stone and Webster Journal*, 361, 365, 1916.

of the 175 cities in which jitneys competed with trolleys. Most major municipalities acted similarly within another year.

The elimination of the jitney industry certainly benefited the electric trolleys, but it also benefited the taxi industry, which we present as another example of restricted competition.

In most cities in the United States, not just anyone can legally drive a taxi, and those who legally do drive a taxi are restricted in many ways in their operation. Most importantly, they are restricted to specific geographic areas and in the price they charge a customer. That price is generally regulated by a commission and is uniform at all times of day for all taxis.

In the taxi business in many cities the potential owner-operator of a cab must purchase what is called a medallion. The ownership of this medallion gives the owner the legal right to operate a taxi within a specified area. So far so good. However, the price of these medallions has at times gone up to $30,000 in New York City and has reached similarly astronomical heights in other cities. How, you might ask, could the right to operate a taxicab cost so much? Clearly, the medallion is inexpensive to produce, even if it is made out of bronze.

The key to understanding this issue is understanding that there are generally a *fixed* number of medallions available. In other words, entry into the taxicab business in many cities in the United States is limited by law to zero. That is the only reason that a medallion owner could sell his rights to taxicab operation to another person for such a high figure. The other person buying the medallion would be unwilling to pay such a price unless he was fairly certain that no new competition would exist in the future and that present monopoly rates of return or profits would continue into the indefinite future for any owner of a medallion. Naturally, those monopoly profits can only exist so long as the monopoly exists, and in a situation in which potential entry merely involves putting a sign on a four-door sedan reading "Taxi for Hire," the possibility of competition eliminating any monopoly profits is great. Only legislation designed for preventing entry could be effective—that is, the police power of the state must be used to protect the monopoly position of individuals in the taxicab business. The documentation on the legislation perpetuating monopolies in cities such as Los Angeles, Dallas, Forth Worth, Philadelphia, Cleveland, New York, and Chicago is impressive and creates an undeniable case in which a classic situation of restricted entry has existed.

As you might expect, if the number of taxicabs is too severely limited, the potential for cheaters or interlopers in the existing monopoly situation will become great. In fact, the "problem" of illegal or "gypsy" cabs operating in New York City is well known. Apparently officials turn a more or less deaf ear to this problem, recognizing that the limitation on the number of medallions has become too severe given the growing population of that city. The same is true of Chicago, where the gypsies are occasionally picked up but only fined $100. In general, there seems to be more toleration of illegal taxicabs in ghetto areas of New York, St. Louis, Pittsburgh, and perhaps Chicago. In such areas there is a demand for taxis because of the diffuse home-work situations. Moreover, there is a relatively large supply of illegal taxicab and taxicab operators because of the large number of unemployed individuals living in those sections who know how to drive.

Often it is suggested that eliminating urban transportation problems would involve the elimination of restrictions against jitneys and against the proliferation of taxis by removing any legislation prohibiting individuals from going into business for themselves. Note, however, that there would be windfall losses suffered by all current owners of taxi licenses. After all, those who benefited from restriction on entry into the business were the *original* owners of the licenses or the monopoly rights. The current owners had to pay a competitive price to obtain those rights, and that competitive price included all of the future stream of monopoly profits that the original owners perceived would exist. Hence current owners only make a normal rate of return. They would suffer losses because the valuable asset —the medallion—which they purchased at a price of, say, $25,000, would then be worth zero. One possibility is for all restrictions on taxicab and jitney operation in certain cities to be lifted while current owners of monopoly rights be compensated for their windfall losses. If this were to occur, it might be that the urban transportation mess could be ameliorated though certainly not solved.

19

THE ECONOMICS OF
OIL SPILLS

In March 1967 the oil tanker *Torrey Canyon* foundered off the southern coast of England, spilling 119,000 tons of crude oil. The resulting slick quickly spread across nearby waters and subsequently blanketed large areas of adjoining English and French coasts. The British government alone spent $8 million on cleanup; and that was only a portion of total cleanup costs. In addition, there was extensive loss of marine life and fouling of beaches and coastlines.

This disaster drew widespread attention because of the extent of the damage it caused. People were suddenly made aware of the threat posed by modern supertankers with capacities now ranging up to 300,000 tons and tankers of 750,000 tons announced. There is even talk of a 1.25 million tonner. The size of these ships is mind-boggling and the amount of oil that they carry awesome. Since most ships are typically fueled by oil, the threat of spillage is not limited to tank ships and barges. In addition to accidents, spills can also result from leaks in transferring oil, from the deliberate pumping out of bilges, and from blowouts of offshore wells, as in the Santa Barbara case.[1] In 1974 there were 26 major oil spills (11 in U.S. waters) topped by the supertanker Metulla off the southern tip of South America with a spill of 26 million gallons of oil. Since oil is not biodegradable (does not deteriorate rapidly), the oceans of the world are accumulating an ever-increasing mass of "indigestible" petroleum; slicks and globules of oil are visible throughout the high seas of the world. The biological consequences are still indeterminate—we simply do not know what the long-run effects on marine life will be. But anybody who has walked the beaches barefoot has had no trouble discovering the fouling consequences on coastlines.

Moreover the problem is complicated by the crisis in petroleum supplies that has resulted from the successful cartel activities of the oil-exporting countries (see Chapter 17). The price of oil rose from approximately $3 a barrel before the Yom Kippur War to over $11 in 1976. The result of this price increase predictably has been to encourage new sources of supply, particularly offshore drilling, to accelerate the construction of a pipeline across Alaska for North Slope oil, and encourage even more giant tankers to bring in oil. Already a major controversy has emerged over the bringing of North Slope oil to markets. Should it be brought by tanker through the Straits of Juan de Fuca and into Puget Sound? A spill from a supertanker in those confined waters would be a major disaster to this region.

Some technological methods have already evolved for cleaning up the mess, and better ones can be devised in the future. But it may prove far less costly to society to prevent future spills effectively. Several alternatives can be considered.

---

[1] The focus of this chapter is on oil spills directly into water. An additional problem is posed by oil spills on land—intentional or accidental—from pipelines, disposal of used oil from 230,000 gasoline stations, etc. Eventually such oil seeps into streams, rivers, lakes, and oceans.

One proposed solution is simply to prohibit offshore drilling and the transportation of petroleum products by water. This would certainly reduce oil spills, but it might lead to undesirable side effects for various sectors of the community. The short-run effects would be a reduction in the supply of crude oil and a resultant rise in the price of all petroleum products. Rich and poor alike use gasoline, but it represents a larger proportion of the expenditures of the poor.[2] Hence a greater burden would fall on low-income groups. The long-run consequences of such a policy are somewhat more difficult to determine. A rise in the price of petroleum products would increase the profitability of new domestic discoveries and thereby lead to more intensive exploration. Whether this would increase the supply sufficiently to cause the price to fall to earlier levels is doubtful.

Moreover, even such a drastic measure taken by the United States would not completely solve the problem, because other nations' tankers would still carry oil and continue to foul the oceans. Since our legal authority extends only a short distance out to sea, our beaches would still not be safe from wandering oil slicks.

It is clearly possible to eliminate most ecological problems by simply shutting off any economic activity that has costs to "innocent bystanders" (*external diseconomies*). But this is usually a prohibitively expensive solution. The number of economic activities with external diseconomies is constantly growing, and totally forbidding such activities would result in a drastic fall in living standards. Can we, then, eliminate the bulk of these side effects without eliminating the economic activity that produces them? These baneful effects exist for one reason: The individuals or groups who create the costs do not bear even a small fraction of them. If the polluting firm had to

[2] Studies have shown the following distribution of gasoline expenditure as a proportion of income: $3000–5000 income, 3.4 percent; $5000–7000 income, 3.3 percent; $7000–15,000 income, less than 2 percent; above $15,000, 1.4 percent.

bear its full social costs, it would be in its interest to eliminate as many as is economic.[3]

In short, one pat answer to most pollution questions is to make the polluter pay. But to do so, we are going to have to alter property rights—that is, change existing laws about ownership. Rights to property must be revised to include the costs as well as the benefits of any attendant economic activity. To cite only two polluters, this would make motorists and pulp-mill operators liable for the air and water pollution they cause.

Implicit in such a course would be the problem of determining the true economic costs of the side effects of certain activities. For example, how is a price tag to be put on the destruction caused by pollution from a steel-mill's smokestacks? In principle, a price can be figured out. But in practice the task is far from simple and is compounded by the problem of effectively assessing the cost against the actual polluter.

This latter point is particularly thorny in the case of oil spills, since the ocean (and frequently even the beaches) are not private property. They are a *common-property resource*, which means that no one owns them, and that everyone can use them. If somebody did own them, he would do what any other property owner does when damaged; he would sue the polluter for the full extent of the damages. This points to one direction that public policy can take.

Lawmakers, however, do not usually think in terms of property rights, but rather in terms of required safety devices or outright prohibitions. Faced with the imminent arrival of oil from Alaska, the state of Washington has been grappling with ways to reduce the likelihood of oil spills in Puget Sound. It passed a "tanker" law in 1975 which required that tankers of more than 50,000 dead-weight tons would have to use a pilot in the waters of Puget Sound. Further, the law barred tankers of more than 125,000 dead-weight tons from entering the Sound and prohibited any tanker of between 40,000 and 125,000 dead-

---

[3] It is easy for people to assert that *all* pollution should be stopped; but the economy will have less real income if the costs of total elimination of pollution exceed the benefits.

weight tons from entering the sound unless it was escorted by tugs or equipped with twin screws, collision-avoidance radar, and a double bottom. Atlantic Richfield Company challenged the law. A three-judge panel did, in fact, strike it down. Their decision will probably be taken to the U.S. Supreme Court. The issue is still undecided. One proposal is to require that all tankers be double-hulled. Still another alternative has been to establish a traffic control system analogous to the air traffic control that now controls commercial aircraft movements. Plans are also under way to establish a tanker port in the straits of Juan de Fuca outside Puget Sound and then have a pipeline to connect with oil refiners in the sound. Such a tanker port would be coupled with either an outright prohibition of large tankers in the sound or a prohibitive tax (say, $10 a barrel) for tanker movements in the sound. Are these policies preferable to making the polluter liable? In part, the answer depends on whether the liability is limited or unlimited.

If liability is limited, then the small tank barge may be discouraged from operating, while the owners of the 300,000-ton tanker will take their chances. Here's why. Say that liability for oil spills could not exceed $100,000. If a small 50,000-ton independent tanker spilled its load, it could mean financial ruin or at least crippling losses for the company. But if a 300,000-ton supertanker from Atlantic Richfield were to break apart, the maximum liability assessment would be a far lighter penalty relative to the potential profits from that superload of oil. Under any given profitability of foundering, the supertanker will sail because potential profits are large enough to warrant risking a spillage fine. The small, one-ship company has no such comfortable assurance. Therefore, in order for the laws to be effective against oil spills, they must contain unlimited-liability clauses.

What would be the result of such laws? Oil carriers would be forced to carry insurance sufficient to cover damages. The high costs of such coverage would probably eliminate giant tankers from some enclosed waters such as Puget Sound or Chesapeake Bay, where the potential liability from a major oil spill would be of immense magnitude. Insurance premiums would decline with improvements in safety devices designed to prevent accidental oil spillage. Operators would therefore be encouraged to install such measures. There would also be an incentive to improve the technology of cleaning up oil spills and thereby to reduce the costs of damages. The suggested program would undoubtedly raise the price of petroleum products to consumers, since all of these alternatives would increase costs.

Such state, national, and international legislation would not solve all the problems connected with oil spills. As in the cases of narcotics and crime (Chapters 4 and 24), one challenge must always be the detection and identification of the culprit. A "finder's fee" for reporting polluters might provide some assistance. The above suggestions point toward a solution common to many ecological dilemmas—property rights will have to be realigned if private and social costs (and benefits) are to coincide. As long as individuals, firms, or even governmental units can foist some of the costs of their actions onto others, they will be human enough to do so. But if reorganized property rights can force the polluter to bear the full costs of his actions, he will have every incentive to act responsibly.

THE ECONOMICS OF
CLAMMING
AND
OTHER "FREE" GOODS

The razor clam (*Siliqua patula*) is a large bivalve from the *Solenidae* family that inhabits the ocean beaches of the Pacific Coast from California to Alaska. Once a major staple of the coastal Indian population, it is now a major prey of the white man escaping the city for the ocean beaches. (Cleaned, cut into steaks, dipped in batter, fried one minute to the side, and served with a bottle of dry white wine, it is superb.)

These clams are dug on minus tides, and the beach area they inhabit is not, at least in the state of Washington, private property. Therefore, access is available to everyone, and the only costs of digging them are cut fingers and an occasional dunking in icy water. Nobody owns them; they are a common-property resource, a "free good." But this fact does not make clams any less subject to economic analysis than goods with price tags on them. A demand schedule exists for clamming. Like other demand schedules, it shows that more people will use more of the product at a low price than at a high one; and that how *much* more they use will depend on how elastic their demand is (that is, how responsive to a given change in price). When the price is zero, as in clamming, the amount used will certainly be much more than at any level of positive price. Again, how much more depends on the elasticity of the demand schedule.

We can also derive, hypothetically at least, a supply curve, although to discover positive prices we would have to envision private ownership of beaches and see how many clams would be offered by beach owners at various prices. The higher the price, the more would be offered. Presumably, if the price were right, the owner would incur costs of "cultivating" and protecting clam beds to increase their yield.

If a market situation existed, an equilibrium price and quantity could be established; but since a wide gap is inevitable between the amount demanded at zero price and the amount supplied at zero price, some device must ration the product. State authorities take on this task, by setting daily catch limits and closing certain seasons to clamming. Current regulations for the state of Washington allow noncommercial diggers to take fifteen clams a day on any ocean beach from midnight to noon between March 16 and June 30. What we have described is unfortunately only a short-run solution. In the dim and distant past when the Pacific Coast was sparsely settled, no particular problem existed (in fact, no limit of season was set, since in those days even at a zero price the supply exceeded the demand).[1] But each year more and more people have more income for traveling to beaches and more leisure to devote to clamming. The result is that the demand keeps increasing, and each year happy clam hunters crowd the minus-tide beaches thicker than sand-fleas. In Oregon the clam-seeking camper sometimes faces lines as much as a mile long.

The supply may also increase if new beaches are opened up or the State Fisheries Department attempts to cultivate more clams on existing beaches. But the increase can be only mini-

[1] By 1925, regulations did limit commercial harvesting of Washington razor clams to the months of March, April, and May. A well-trained clam digger can remove as much as half a ton of clams during one low tide, but there was no need then to restrict the season for noncommercial clam digging.

mal, once all the beaches have been made accessible. The result must inevitably be more crowding and fewer clams, year by year. It is not a happy prospect.

The clamming story is repeated over and over again for recreational activities, and the same analysis applies. In the case of wilderness areas, the supply is actually decreasing rather than merely remaining constant. Fishing, hunting, and camping sites are overcrowded, although these have somewhat greater potential for expansion of supply.

What is being done to improve the situation? A price is charged for fishing and hunting, in the form of license fees, and more recently camping sites in parks are being "rented." In each case, however, the rates have been set so far below the equilibrium price which could balance quantities supplied with quantities demanded that they are not even close to resolving the issue. And each year it gets worse. Anyone wanting to test the proposition need only visit Yellowstone or Yosemite National Park in the summer.

Contrast the case of clams with those oyster beds in the state of Washington that were privately owned before the state restricted private ownership of tidal land. Here the oyster beds were treated as an asset in which investment was made to improve the yield. In fact, oysters are farmed just like any other agricultural commodity. Perhaps the most spectacular contrast is that between the north and south shore of Chesapeake Bay. On the north shore, the state of Maryland has made the oyster beds a common property resource and as would be expected where entry was unlimited, severe depletion has occurred. Moreover, it has not been worthwhile to privately invest in improving the yield. In order to cut down on the harvest, the state has forced the use of archaic harvesting tools and archaic propulsion requirements (that is, oyster dredging can only be done under sail power). In contrast, the state of Virginia on the south shore has had private ownership of tidal lands. With 80 percent of the tidal land in private hands, owners have developed the oyster beds into a thriving sustained enterprise. The average output per worker was 59 percent higher in

Virginia than in Maryland during the 25 year period 1945–1969.[2]

Why are we content with a zero price for clamming, or with only a nominal fee for fishing? The answer is that the American people have long believed that such activities are a hereditary right, that they should be equally accessible to rich and poor alike, and that charging a fee favors the rich (which it certainly does). This argument prevails in the cases of clamming, fishing, and hunting, but not in the case of buying yachts and airplanes. The result is to lower artificially the price for a particular publicly owned commodity—clams—but not for all commodities. In effect, the public policy is saying that income should not be a factor in people's ability to clam or to fish, but that it can be one in buying golf clubs, TV sets, or airplanes. That is, in effect, a policy of selective income redistribution—a subject to be examined in the final chapters of this book.

As crowding, rationing, and queuing become more and more severe in such nonpriced or underpriced activities, it becomes a major issue to determine whether rationing by price or by quantity restriction is the better method. One alternative is to eliminate the common-property aspects of such resources. Another is for the government to set a price that approximates a market price. The final alternative consists of a variety of rationing devices to restrict quantity more and more rigidly.

[2] Richard J. Agnello and Lawrence P. Donnelley, "Property Rights and Efficiency in the Oyster Industry," *Journal of Law and Economics*, vol. 18, no. 2 (October 1975), p. 531.

THE ECONOMICS OF
HONEY

You can buy apple blossom honey, blueberry blossom honey, cranberry blossom honey, alfalfa honey, red clover honey, fireweed honey, mint honey, sage honey, orange honey, even cabbage honey. We all know how honey is made: Bees suck out the nectar from various blossoms and it is transformed, via one of nature's most useful processes, into the honey you buy in the store. In many states there are large bee farms, with hives generally consisting of one or two brood chambers, a queen excluder, and from zero to six supers. A brood chamber is a big wooden box large enough to contain eight or ten movable frames. Each frame will have a wax honeycomb built by the bees. It is in the hexagonal cells of this comb that the queen will lay her eggs and the young bees, or brood, will be raised. The bees store the nectar and pollen, which they use for food. Honey is usually not extracted from this chamber but from the frames of a shallower box, which we call a super, placed above the brood chamber. The queen excluder is placed between the super, which is used only for honey, and the brood chamber, which is used only for raising young bees. The excluder prevents the queen from laying eggs in the upper section of the hive.

Beekeepers and bees work according to a cycle that runs through the year. During part of the year, usually from spring to fall, the colony of bees will hatch continuously. The infants are raised on pollen, and they remain in the brood for about three weeks before starting to do any work. Worker bees spend the first three weeks of their working life helping clean and repair the wax cells in the brood and nursing the young. For the remainder of their lives, usually two to three more weeks, they look around for pollen and nectar.

During the spring, bees are at their busiest when they are pollinating fruit trees, for at that time the infants must be fed with nectar and pollen. Fruit-tree owners obviously benefit by having honey bees nearby, for they will enjoy a larger yield per acre because of the pollination services the bees provide. Here we have a classic situation that in the economic literature has been labeled an *externality*. In 1952, the economist J. E. Meade pointed out that applying more labor, land, and capital to apple farming will not only increase the output of apples, but will also provide more food for the bees. Meade called this a case "of an unpaid factor, because the situation is due simply and solely to the fact that the apple farmer cannot charge the beekeeper for the bees' food. . . ."[1]

We can look at the situation from the other side of the coin: The apple trees may provide food for the bees, but the bees also fertilize the apple blossoms. If the beekeeper in the vicinity of the apple trees increases the size of his or her colony, he or she presumably foresees the increased benefit only as the additional revenues to be received from a larger honey supply that can be sold. At the same time, though, the apple farmer will receive a benefit in the form of a higher pollination rate of apple blossoms and, hence, a higher supply of apples at the end of the season. Again we have a situation of an unpaid factor, an externality. There are benefits external to both the decision made by the apple farmer and the decision made by the beekeeper.

[1] J. E. Meade, "External Economies and Diseconomies in a Competitive Situation," *Economic Journal* (March 1952), pp. 56–57.

In classic economic analysis, an externality is associated with what is called a *market failure*. That is, the private market fails to allocate resources in an efficient manner. The apple and bee example has been used in economics for many years now to demonstrate an externality situation in which the government should step in and correct the relative prices in order to take account of benefits that the apple farmer and the beekeeper apparently do not perceive, or at least cannot charge for.

Only recently has someone taken the time to find out if the quaint apple-farmer-beekeeper example actually exists in the real world around us. Besides the fact that apple blossoms yield little or no honey, apparently both beekeepers and fruit growers do understand that bees provide valuable pollination services. Moreover, beekeepers and fruit growers realize that plants will provide valuable honey crops. Once it is understood by at least one of the parties in question that a valuable external benefit occurs as a result of his or the other's action, we would expect some attempt to be made at taking advantage of this knowledge. That attempt would translate itself into a contractual arrangement between the fruit grower and the beekeeper. Contracts are not a new invention; they have existed since the beginning of social relations among humans. We all know certain types of contracts, such as the kind made with a bank in order to take out a loan. But contracts are not limited to obvious endeavors. In fact, contracts exist, either explicitly or implicitly, for an incredibly large number of economic and even noneconomic transactions. We can cite a marriage contract, an employment contract, an educational contract—a contract for just about every action known to man. The beekeepers and the fruit and plant growers, therefore, could be expected to figure out a contract between them that would take account of the so-called externalities involved in each one's behavior.

We find conclusive evidence that both nectar and pollination services are indeed contracted for and transacted in the marketplace. In many cases, all we have to do is look in the Yellow Pages. We find there an entry called "pollination ser-

Bee-Related Plants Investigated in the State of Washington, 1971

Plants	Number of Beekeepers	Pollination Services Rendered	Surplus Honey Expected	Approximate Season	Number of Hives per Acre (Range)
Fruits & Nuts					
Apple & soft fruits[a]	7	Yes	No	Mid-April–Mid-May	0.4 to 2
Blueberry (with maple)	1	Yes	Yes	May	2
Cherry (early)	1	Yes	No	March–Early April	0.5 to 2
Cherry	2	Yes	No	April	0.5 to 2
Cranberry	2	Yes	Negligible	June	1.5
Almond (Calif.)	2	Yes	No	February–March	2
Legumes					
Alfalfa	5	Yes and No[c]	Yes	June–September	0.3 to 3
Red clover	4	Yes and No	Yes	June–September	0.5 to 5
Sweet clover	1	No[d]	Yes	June–September	0.5 to 1
Pasture[b]	4	No	Yes	Late May–September	0.3 to 1
Other Plants					
Cabbage	1	Yes	Yes	Early April–May	1
Fireweed	2	No	Yes	July–September	n.a.
Mint	3	No	Yes	July–September	0.4 to 1

[a] Soft fruits include pears, apricots, and peaches.
[b] Pasture includes a mixture of plants, notably the legumes and other wild flowers such as dandelions.
[c] Pollination services are rendered for alfalfa and the clovers if their seeds are intended to be harvested; when they are grown only for hay, hives will still be employed for nectar extraction.
[d] Sweet clover may also require pollination services, but such a case is not covered by this investigation.
Source: See footnote 2, p. 148.

vices." Whereas economists for many years have felt that "the apple farmer cannot charge the beekeeper for the bees' food and the beekeeper cannot charge the apple farmer for the bees' pollination services," such is not the case. Not only can the respective parties charge for the services they render, but they actually do, and some of them make a very good business of it. In a study done in the state of Washington,[2] it was found that about 60 beekeepers each owned 100 colonies or more. During the peak season the total colonies' strength was about 90,000 bees. Beekeepers would relocate hives from farm to farm by trucking them. Thus, beekeepers not only could render pollination services to different fruit and plant owners at different times of the year, but could extract different types of honey at different times of the year as well. On average, a hive in Washington State took care of two and one-half crops a year. The accompanying table shows that sometimes beekeepers provided pollination services and sometimes they didn't; sometimes plant owners provided honey services and sometimes they didn't.

When we look at what beekeepers charge for pollination services, we find an interesting but not wholly unexpected phenomenon: The greater the expected honey yield, the smaller the pollination fee. Essentially then, beekeepers will be paid in kind rather than in money for the pollination services they render to plant owners. Moreover, the more effort the beekeepers put into dispersing their hives throughout the orchard, the more they charge for their services, because pollination improves with increased dispersal of hives.

So here we have a situation where an elusive resource, a flying insect, renders services to the owner of another resource. A very specific type of contract has been drawn up for these circumstances, in order to take account of any benefits obtained. These contracts take both oral and written form. In the state of Washington, a printed one is issued by the Association of Beekeepers. A contract need not be in writing, however,

[2] S. N. S. Cheung, "The Fable of the Bees: An Economic Investigation," *Journal of Law and Economics* (April 1973).

even in a court of law. In any event, oral contracts will generally not be broken when information can travel very quickly about who broke one and why. This is exactly the situation in the society of beekeepers and farmers in which everyone knows everyone else and knows his past reputation as well. A glance at the written pollination contracts reveals stipulations concerning the number and strength of the colonies, the time of delivery of the hives and the time of their removal, what will be done to protect the bees from pesticides, how the hives should be placed, and the cost of each hive's services.

Whenever there are gains to be made from contracting among different parties in an economic system, so long as the cost of making and enforcing the contract is less than the gains, we will generally observe a contract being made, even if only an oral one. This is true even where natural resources are concerned. Thus the classic economist's example of an externality turns out not to be one at all. It does provide us, though, with valuable clues to when and where externalities will exist. In the case of the bees, contracting was profitable for the parties concerned; in the cases of automobile pollution, the High Mountain Sheep Dam, or Bristol Bay salmon, the costs of negotiating and enforcing contracts exceed the gains. This is so because we do not have any cheap (efficient) way to measure, define, and enforce property rights over dirty air, scenic beauty, and fish swimming in the ocean.

THE ECONOMICS OF FLOODING HELL'S CANYON

Hell's Canyon, on the Snake River separating Oregon from Idaho, is the deepest canyon on the North American continent, exceeding even the Grand Canyon. It offers some of the most spectacular scenery in the country; it is a natural habitat for elk, deer, and bighorn sheep; the hillsides echo to the call of vast flocks of redleg partridge; and the rushing river contains salmon, steelhead, and sturgeon.

Hell's Canyon is also perhaps the best remaining site in the United States for developing hydroelectric power. The results of such a development would be a high dam which would turn the river into a huge lake, backing it all the way up to an already existing dam and lake farther up the river.

Should this new dam be built?

The issue created a controversy that has continued for many years. During this time the plans and proposed sites for the dam have changed. The protagonists on either side have also changed (in some cases they have even changed sides). And what was once a controversy between public and private power over two alternative and mutually exclusive dam sites has become a debate between those who want no dam at all and the unified forces of the public and private power groups who contended that the dam should be constructed and operated by their joint efforts.

While rhetoric and power politics dominated the headlines, the issue was fought before the Federal Power Commission with numbers. The numbers were plugged into benefit-cost analyses of the dam; and, since several alternative dam combinations were proposed, alternative benefit-cost analyses were developed. We shall look at just one—the High Mountain Sheep Dam, clearly the most impressive hydroelectric proposal.

Benefit-cost analysis has been developed to help determine the social as distinguished from the private profitability of economic activities. What's the difference? For the production of a vast array of goods and services there is either no difference, or one so little that no one bothers about it. In such cases, the private opportunity costs of the amount of capital and the expected returns dictate whether to undertake an economic activity. For instance, if a predicted rate of return exceeds the opportunity cost of capital for a proposed factory, the factory will be built.

However, where externalities exist—that is, where benefits or costs accrue to persons other than the investor (and the user)—the purely private calculation may yield the wrong decision from the viewpoint of society as a whole. In the case of the High Mountain Sheep Dam project, a private investor undertaking the project would not get the benefits of the additional power that could be generated at downstream power plants as a result of regulating the flow of the river and releasing more water at periods of low-stream flow. Nor would a private investor reap the benefits from reducing flood damage in the lower Snake and Columbia rivers as a result of reducing stream flow in periods of high water and potential flooding. On the other hand, neither would that investor bear the costs to society of destroying or damaging the runs of migratory fish; reducing wildlife habitat, both waterfowl and mammal; and irrevocably altering the scenic beauty of a unique and irreplaceable area.

Some of these externalities are relatively easy to measure. One is the downstream benefits of a dam, which are simply the value of the additional power generated times the price per kilowatt-hour. Another is the value of reduced flood damage, which can be calculated by assessing how much damage could be done downstream by the amount of water to be stored and multiplying that by the frequency with which such high water would occur in the absence of the dam (this data being obtainable from historical river records). But who can measure the externalities involved in the destruction of the aesthetic grandeur and recreational value of a previously undeveloped canyon? Let's see how this calculation was attempted in the case of High Mountain Sheep Dam.

Omitting, for the moment, the external costs associated with altering the environment, opponents of the dam measured all other costs and benefits of the proposed dam versus the next-best alternative, which was nuclear power. They then asked what value would have to be placed on preservation of the original environment to justify *not* building the dam.[1] The conclusion was that over its projected 50-year life span, the High Mountain Sheep Dam would provide benefits over its next-best alternative of between $14 and $24 million, depending on assumptions made about other dams and the nuclear alternative.

A brief resumé of the way the figures were derived will illustrate the usual procedure in such cases. The total investment cost of the dam with an interest rate of 9 percent was calculated at $266,786,000. That is, bonds would be floated at that interest rate to provide that sum. This brought the total annual costs (fixed charges on the bonds, plus costs for operating, generating, and transmission) to $39,597,000.

On the benefit side, the power benefits (presumably including downstream benefits) were $41,894,000 annually and the

---

[1] The following data are drawn from Dr. John Krutilla's testimony before the Federal Power Commission.

flood-control benefits were $245,000 annually, for a total of $42,139,000. Gross annual costs subtracted from gross annual benefits thus leave a net benefit of $2,542,000 annually. This comes to $24,068,000 over the 50-year life span of the project.

The last figure should bother you: A net annual benefit of $2.5 million multiplied by 50 years comes to a lot more than $24 million. Or does it? No, because a dollar earned today is considerably more valuable than a dollar earned next year, and about 75 times as valuable as a dollar earned 50 years hence. The reason for this is really quite simple. We must ask how many of today's dollars will be needed to make $2.5 million next year, recognizing that today's dollars can earn perhaps 9 percent (that is, their opportunity costs and the rate at which we *discount* future dollars). A few simple calculations will convince you that the present value of $2.5 million 50 years from now (that is, the number of today's dollars needed to provide $2.5 million at 9 percent annual compound interest) is not that great. So the further away the benefit in time and the higher the opportunity cost of money (the interest rate), the lower the present value. The same reasoning applies to costs. When all the arithmetic is worked out, $24 million appears as the upper-bound estimate. The lower-bound estimate of $14 million was calculated in similar fashion using a different interest (discount) rate.

Now we come to the critical question. Is the value of preserving the existing canyon equal to $14–24 million over the next 50 years? How do you measure the enjoyment of a natural scenic attraction? The ideal answer would be obtained by assessing what people would be willing to pay to maintain the canyon. We have no answer, but we can get a little closer by some indirect methods. We find that in Norway, for example, where streams can be owned privately, sports fishermen are willing to pay as much as $500 a day for fishing rights in certain Atlantic salmon stream areas. Since the steelhead is a close cousin of the Atlantic salmon, we can get some notion of the value people place upon such fishing in the Hell's Canyon. Canadian Atlantic salmon leasing prices give further information. We can also attempt to discover how willing people have been to pay for hunting and other forms of recreation under market conditions by similar means.

Furthermore, it is clear that the value of recreational resources is growing each year, as increased income and leisure time enable more and more people to enjoy such facilities. Since the demand is increasing at all prices but the supply is fixed,[2] the value will inevitably keep rising. Overall, by such approximations, the authors of the rebuttal study for High Mountain Sheep Dam concluded that the recreational benefits of the original canyon do indeed surpass the $14–24 million of benefits to be expected from hydroelectric development.

When we wrote the first edition of this book the issue was still in doubt. Now it is settled. Was it resolved by cold benefit-cost calculus? Hardly! While the figures undoubtedly had some influence, the final determination was made in the political arena by Congress, which passed a law prohibiting further dam construction on that portion of the Snake River.

[2] Theoretically, substitutes do exist, but it is not clear how close they really are.

THE ECONOMICS OF
LAND USE

A growing population with a fixed supply of land has produced some classic problems in our economic past, several of which we have dealt with in other editions of this book. A growth in the supply of one factor of production in the face of a fixed supply of all others yields diminishing returns to the former in the absence of any other changes. We have seen, however, in the case of resources that this problem, at least in the short run, has been resolved by technology, which has made us more productive in using a fixed amount of land. In this chapter we see another aspect of the problems of growing population (together with growing income) and a fixed land supply, and that is what is commonly called suburban sprawl. It is characterized by a landscape of unsightly billboards, vast junk piles of old automobiles, neon jungles of lights along the roadways and freeways. It is obvious that the unplanned expansion of population into and through the countryside produces visual external diseconomies of monumental proportions. It produces other kinds of undesirable externalities when a factory is built in the middle of a residential area, a noxious-smelling pulp mill is built upwind from where people live, or a smelter emits sulfur dioxide into the air, which drops through rainfall into surrounding territories. The growing problem of land use and how to control land use poses a major social problem today.

The state of California has pioneered a comprehensive attempt to do something about one aspect of this problem, the coastal area of the state. An initiative called the Coastal Zone Conservation Act was passed on November 7, 1972. The act set up a coastal zone defined as the area from as far out to sea as the state had legal jurisdiction to as far inland as the highest elevation of the closest mountain range. This coastal zone extends from southern border to northern border. Moreover, all the land within the zone, anywhere from the high tide to 1,000 yards inland, was designated as a "permit" area where any use of that land could not be engaged in unless a permit was obtained from a regional coastal commission. Therefore, starting some time in 1973, owners of land in the permit area could engage in no construction without going through a hearing to obtain (hopefully) a permit. According to the initiative, such legislation was deemed necessary: "The people of the state of California hereby find and declare that the California Coastal Zone is a distinct and valuable natural resource belonging to all the People."

The Coastal Zone Conservation Act in California is more comprehensive but still symptomatic of a burgeoning series of legislation all subsumed under the title "Land Use Law." Although apparently new in title, land use laws certainly have been around a long time. We all are familiar with zoning ordinances, the first one being adopted by New York City in 1916 to prevent the garment district from expanding into the fashionable Fifth Avenue shopping area. Practically all cities in the United States have zoning ordinances that restrict the use of land to various categories. Land that is zoned residential cannot, in principle, be used for construction of a factory. Land that is zoned light residential cannot be used, in principle, for heavy industrial applications. In some states land that is zoned agricultural cannot be turned into residential areas. Zoning laws or local land use laws are often cited as necessary in order to prevent the disorderly growth of a community. Supporters of zoning contend that without it factories would be built in residential areas, thus ruining them for the residents, or, as another example, without zoning, homes could be turned into offices, thus creating problems for neighbors. A new Act was passed in 1976 giving increased powers to the California Coastal Zone Conservation Commission.

The extent of such mixed use in the absence of zoning is controversial. In Houston, Texas, where no zoning ordinances exist, the results are surprising. It turns out that in Houston factories remain with factories, offices remain with offices, and houses remain with houses. Moreover, expensive houses do not seem to be mingled with inexpensive houses and vice versa. One student of the Houston situation ran the following experiment: He presented to various city planners unnamed city maps showing industrial areas, residential areas, and so on. Included in the sample were Houston, without zoning, and a number of America's major cities which are heavily zoned. Without fail, none of the city planners could pick out the plan of that city—Houston—which had never been zoned! Strangely enough (or not so strangely, as we will see) Houston, without zoning, has developed just like cities with zoning. How could that be? It is economically unwise (i.e., not very profitable) for a group of entrepreneurs to purchase expensive residential land on which to build a factory. Why? Because it is usually cheaper to purchase less expensive land where factories already exist or where no residences have yet been built. In other words, land that is suitable for residences is generally not suitable for factories because it is too expensive, and a potential home builder certainly does not need to be told not to put up a house in a smelly industrial area.

Moreover, businesspersons wishing to rent office space certainly will not pay much for an office in the middle of an industrial complex, nor would it make sense to purchase office space in the middle of a residential neighborhood. After all, there are certain economies to being grouped together with other offices and thereby making it profitable for services that cater to office needs to be readily available in the immediate vicinity. Just to cite a simple example, consider the profitability of setting up a copying company in the middle of a residential area that happened to contain a few offices as opposed to doing the same thing in a downtown area where numerous offices existed or were going to exist. Adam Smith once said that specialization depends on the size of the market. For factories and offices, more specialization is possible the greater the concentration of the market in one area. Hence we generally see similar types of economic activity being carried on in fairly well defined areas within a community.

Nevertheless, this description of rational market allocation of land use as characterized by the city of Houston in the absence of zoning laws does not do away with the problem we posed at the beginning of this chapter. Anyone who has wandered through the countryside of the United States, or indeed compared it with the English or Swiss countrysides, cannot help but be struck by the striking contrast between the two. Yet by now we are all familiar enough with economics to understand that the issues are more controversial than either the town planner from England or the devoted advocate of the free market would like to believe. Specifically, we can see some of the problems by drawing out the implications of the dilemma that the California coastal plan leads to. In this case the regional commissions have the power to deny all practical use of land within the permit area. What has happened then in California is a transference in decision-making about the use of land from the owner of land to a commission of individuals who have no personal stake in the property under question. This raises two fundamental and very difficult problems. The first of these concerns how the commission decides on the proper allocation of resources: What criteria do they use, and what is good land use? The market gives a set of signals, however wrong they may be in cases where significant externalities exist. Nevertheless, it is a set of signals that are clear and unambiguous, but the conflicting interests and concerns and pressures of citizens over land use as empowered in the commissioners are something else again. Slogans like "in the interest of the people" or "in the interests of a majority of the people," familiar to us in the political rhetoric of such policies, are not a guide to policy. This is one dilemma and a major one. The second fundamental problem is the transference of wealth as a consequence of these policies.

For example, if you were the owner of a piece of land that a regional commission will not allow anything to be built on, except perhaps a putting green, you will have suffered a reduction in your wealth, for that land will be essentially worthless. Your loss will be equal to the value of the land in the use permitted by the regional commission subtracted from the market value of the land before the land use law was passed. Generally, such actions in the past have been construed by the courts as the taking of property from individuals that had to be compensated for by the state. This is contained in the 5th Amendment to the Constitution of the United States. Prior to 1850, the 5th Amendment's "taking clause" was interpreted strictly to mean only the taking in the physical sense of the word. However, in 1922 Justice Oliver Wendell Holmes, Jr., enunciated the view that regulation of land can go far enough to amount to a taking, for which a landowner is therefore entitled to compensation.[1] Obviously, using the interpretation of Holmes would require states to compensate individuals whose land values plummeted because of their inability to use the land in any meaningful way after passage of a land use law.

Environmentalists contend that this interpretation is no longer valid. One of the reasons given is that such an interpretation would require the states to fork over immense sums of money to individuals whose property values suffered because of land use laws. The question at issue here, of course, is who should bear the cost of maintaining an environment, say, for example, along the coast of California, that is devoid of any further multifamily dwellings. Should it be the individual landowners who, when they purchased the land, did not suspect that the Coastal Zone Conservation Act would come into exis-

[1] *Pennsylvania Coal Company* v. *Mohan*, 1922.

tence in 1972, or should it be the taxpayers of the state of California taken as a group?

According to a report issued on August 16, 1973, by the Council on Environmental Quality, it is the property owners who should bear the costs, not the taxpayers.[2] The authors of the report contend that the 5th Amendment "taking clause" should again be interpreted in a strict manner; that is, only if land is physically taken from its owner should the owner be compensated by the state. We certainly cannot conclude from any of the above analyses that the authors are correct or incorrect. We do, however, point out two problems: (1) Generally individuals are required in our society to pay for scarce resources that they use. If undeveloped coastal land gives value to the citizens of a state, presumably they would be willing to pay for that privilege, that is, for the use of the scarce resource called *undeveloped* land. If the state merely passes regulatory land use laws giving the citizens this scarce resource, they then will be receiving a free ride at the expense of the property owners who suffered reductions in their wealth. And (2) It does not appear that there will be any feedback mechanisms by which the individuals giving land use permits will be able to tell whether they are allowing too many or too few multi-family dwellings as opposed to single-family dwellings, or parks as opposed to tennis courts, and so on. It would appear then that an efficient use of the resource in question would be difficult to effect without some feedback mechanism that could in some way or another measure the satisfaction that individuals were receiving from the resource in its different uses.

It has been suggested that a way around some of the above-mentioned problems is to allow decision-making to be done democratically. Take the case of a desirable area in California, say, San Diego. The question arises as to whether or not a certain area around San Diego should be further developed. Let us say that it is now without many dwellings, but rather consists of fruit trees, open areas, and coastline. A group of

[2] F. P. Bosselman, et al., "The Taking Issue: An Analysis of the Constitutional Limits of Land Use Control," Council on Environmental Quality (Washington, D.C.: GPO, 1973).

developers wishes to build single family residences, apartment houses, and condominiums. A referendum is then put to the vote of the public. Should San Diegoans allow further development of the delineated undeveloped area? As you might predict, the vote would (and did!) come out strongly against development. In fact, in the extreme we would imagine that only the developers would vote in favor; everyone else against.

This all sounds democratic, but on closer scrutiny, it is not. Who do the developers represent? Not just themselves, but rather all of those individuals who would like to move to San Diego, but do not at the present time because housing prices are, in their minds, too high. We are talking now about, for example, those people who live in colder climates who want to retire to the milder temperatures in San Diego County. We are talking about people who live in Buffalo, New York, Lansing, Michigan, and St. Paul, Minnesota. Actually, the would-be developers are betting that there are a sufficient number of such people who would indeed want to purchase residences in San Diego County if they were built. But, in a democratic voting system, it is only the San Diego residents who can vote, not all the potential purchasers of new housing in San Diego. Thus, we see that those who benefit from *not* developing certain areas in the county are not really the ones who pay for that benefit. The ones who pay are the ones who decide they cannot afford to move to the warmer climate; but they were not allowed to vote.

We face a dilemma. Many people would like decision-making at the municipal level to be done democratically. But if the vote is used to decide how land is to be used, then we will be almost certain to see the costs borne by those who are not allowed to vote.

24

THE ECONOMICS OF
CRIME PREVENTION

For 1976, New York City chose to permit 1622 murders, 3400 rapes, 77,940 robberies, 195,243 burglaries, and 27,456 assaults, as well as various numbers of lesser crimes.

Stated in other terms, New York City appropriated a sum in excess of $800 million for the police department for that year. We start our examination with an assumption that the amount of resources devoted to crime prevention is inversely correlated to the amount of crime. Had the city of New York appropriated twice that amount, would there have been less crime? How much less? In short, what is the relation between prevention of crime and money spent? How did the city decide on that figure?

Before we can begin to answer these questions, we must look in greater detail at the economics of fighting crime. First of all, it is not only the police and other law-enforcement agencies that are used in crime prevention. The courts and various types of penal and reform institutions also enter the project, as do devices such as burglar alarms, locks, and safes. In total, more than $65 billion was spent to combat crime in the United States in 1977 (about 4 percent of net national product).

Like any other area of complex modern living, criminal law

enforcement has many aspects and the costs of each must be considered in allocating the resources available. First is the detection of a crime (in cases such as narcotics or prostitution) and the arrest of suspects. Next, costs are involved in the trial and conviction of the prisoner; they depend on the efficiency and speed with which the law-enforcement officials and the courts can act. Third, once the sentence is imposed, we are faced with the economic costs of maintaining and staffing prisons. But more important are the social implications of the question: What sorts and durations of punishment are most effective as deterrents to crime? We shall postpone examining this last question of the relationship between crime and punishment until the next chapter. Let's examine the other questions.

The amount of resources devoted to discovering and apprehending criminals is obviously directly related to a reduction in crime. But the optimum allocation of those resources is not so clear-cut. The chief of police or the commissioner is faced by two sets of problems. On the one hand, he or she must decide how to divide the funds between capital and labor— that is, shall he or she choose more cars, equipment, and laboratories; or more police personnel, detectives, and technicians? On the other hand, he or she must also allocate his or her funds among the various police details within the department; for example, he or she could decide whether to clamp down harder on homicide or on car theft.

Within a law-enforcement budget of a given size he or she must, then, determine the optimum combination of production factors. The ideal combination is one in which an additional dollar spent on any one of the labor or capital inputs will provide an equal additional amount of enforcement. If an additional dollar spent on laboratory equipment yields a higher crime-deterrent result than the same dollar spent on a police officer's salary, the laboratory will win. While it is clear that inputs cannot be measured in such small amounts, the question of *indivisibility*[1] or lumpiness in production does not alter the

---

[1] A good or service is said to be indivisible if it can be sold only in relatively large quantities. For example, one cannot purchase one-tenth of a

basic argument. Nor does it alter the argument to recognize that we cannot precisely measure the returns on an increase in labor or in some input of capital. The police captain must normally judge from experience and intuition, as well as from available data, whether buying more cars or hiring more men and women will do the better job in checking crime. And note that his or her decision may change with changes in relative price. For example, when the salaries of police officers are raised, the balance may tip toward the use of more cars or equipment, depending on how well capital can be substituted for labor in a given situation. Instead of using two police officers in a car, it might be economically efficient to equip the car with bulletproof glass and let the driver patrol alone.

The second task of the police chief is to determine how to allocate his or her resources among the interdepartmental details. Sometimes highly publicized events may influence his or her decision. For example, a few years ago, prostitution increased in downtown Seattle to such a degree that local merchants protested vigorously that streetwalkers were hurting business. They had sufficient political influence to induce the police chief to step up sharply the detection and apprehension of prostitutes. That meant using more personnel and equipment on the vice squad; and within the restriction of a fixed budget this could be done only by pulling them from homicide, robbery, and other details, which were thus made short-handed. In effect, the cost of reducing prostitution was a short-run increase in assault and robbery. It is not clear (in the short run, at least) that political pressure of the sort just mentioned leads to a concentration of police enforcement in those areas that many people feel are most essential.

We said that three general areas of law enforcement entail costs to society, and we have just dealt with the area of detection and arrest. The second area is trial and its outcome. Recent studies indicate that the likelihood of conviction is a

police car. However, perhaps the car can be rented for one-tenth of each month. Given the possibility of rental, many products can no longer be called indivisible.

highly important factor (if not the major one) in the prevention of crime. Currently, the probability of conviction and punishment for crime is extremely low in the United States. In New York City, it is estimated that an individual who commits a felony faces less than 1 chance in 200 of going to jail.[2] Lack of detection is one part of the explanation for this incredible figure; court congestion is another. In highly urbanized environments, the court calendar is so clogged that the delay in getting a case to trial may stretch from months into years.[3] One consequence of this situation is an increasing tendency for the prosecutor and suspect to arrange a pretrial settlement rather than further overburden the courts. This is what happens to 80 to 90 percent of criminal charges. The effect on the morale of the police officers who have brought the cases to trial is painfully obvious. Society may be underinvesting in the resources necessary to improve this process. If more were to be spent on streamlining court proceedings instead of concentrating so heavily on making arrests, cases could be brought to trial more promptly, the presence of all witnesses could be more easily secured, and the hand of the D.A. would not be forced in making "deals" with suspects. Faced with the probability of quick and efficient trial, a potential criminal might think harder about robbing a bank or mugging a pedestrian. Chief Justice Warren E. Burger himself has recently declared that we do in fact need an overhauling of our courts.

There remains another issue which is highly controversial. The likelihood of detection and conviction can be increased by new technical means, wiretapping, and by changes in the laws protecting the rights of suspects (e.g., by permitting law officers to enter and search without knocking, lifting the requirement that suspects be informed of their Constitutional rights, and allowing the holding of suspects incommunicado for lengthy periods). However, the costs of such legal changes in

---

[2] *Wall Street Journal*, August 20, 1970.
[3] Many court calendars are solidly booked for 2, 3, or even 5 years into the future. In New York, for example, the average time lapse between filing a civil suit and getting it to trial is 39 months.

terms of infringement on individual liberties are extremely serious, and in any event we do not have the information necessary to determine how effective such changes would be.

We can now return to our original question. How did New York City determine that a budget for crime prevention of in excess of $800 million was the right amount? In the short run, they were faced with a total budget of a given size and had to decide how to carve it up between law enforcement and other municipal demands, such as fire protection, health, parks, streets, and libraries. Just as a police chief can try to determine what combination of police officers and equipment within his fixed budget will deter the greatest amount of crime, a city council will attempt to choose a combination of spending on all agencies that will yield the maximum amount of public services. If additional money spent on fire protection does not yield as much "good" as it would if spent on police protection, then the amount should be allocated to law enforcement.[4] Determining the value of services rendered by each agency of course poses a touchy problem. However, it is not insuperable, at least in principle. We saw in the case of the Hell's Canyon issue (Chapter 22) that crude approximations can be made of the benefits and costs of recreation. This can be applied equally to other nonpriced goods and services, and the efficiency of the public sector of our economy will be improved as such calculations are made and refined.

The short-run constraint of a fixed budget for law enforcement may be altered in the long run by going to the state legislature and asking for increased funds for crime prevention. The legislature then has to wrestle with the same allocation problem that has engaged the city council. Funds can be increased for a city's budget only by tightening the belt in some other area such as school expenditures or park development. The same, now-familiar calculations must now be made on the state level: Will spending an additional dollar on higher education yield greater returns for society than the same dollar

[4] The city council equates on the margin returns from money spent on all municipal activities.

given to a city council to allocate to crime prevention? The same difficult problem arises in measuring the dollar value of nonpriced services resulting from any given state expenditure.

The state does have an option not open to most city councils in most states. It can raise taxes. Now we have widened the allocation problem. The increased taxes will reduce the disposable income of some part of the citizenry. Those who pay the additional taxes must in turn decide whether they feel the additional public services made available are worthwhile. For example, they must decide whether the reduction in crime attributable to an increased expenditure on law enforcement is as valuable to them as the goods they could have enjoyed from that increased tax money. If they do not think so, then at the next election they will vote to "throw the rascals out."

The above description indicates that nonmarket solutions to economic problems run basically parallel to market solutions. Although we have focused on crime prevention, the issues are similar for all types of government decisions and for all levels of government—local, state, and federal.

But certain differences must also be noted between decision-making in the private market sector of the economy and in the public nonmarket sector. Problems of measurement are much greater in the latter. How do we put a price tag on recreation, which is the output of the parks department? For another thing, the signals come through much louder and more clearly in market situations in which changes in private profitability "telegraph" to entrepreneurs what policies will be best.[5] Instead of market signals, the maker of public policy receives a confused set of noises generated by opponents and proponents of his decisions. A legislator is in the unenviable position of trying to please as many of the electorate as possible while operating with very incomplete information.

Some cities have tried to use market mechanisms to improve crime prevention. The city of Orange, California, near Los Angeles, a few years ago started paying its police according to

[5] In instances where externalities exist, it may be to society's advantage to alter these signals by appropriate measures.

how much crime was reduced. The incentive scheme applies to four categories of crime—burglary, robbery, rape, and auto theft. Under the plan, as first put into effect, if the crime rate in those categories was cut by 3 percent for the first 8 months of the year compared with the first 8 months in the previous year, the police would get an extra 1-percent raise. If the crime rate fell by 6 percent, the pay increase would be an extra 2 percent. The results have been encouraging. Detectives on their own time produce video-tape briefings with leads for patrol officers on specific beats. The whole force developed a campaign to encourage safety precautions in residents' homes. Statistically speaking, the results were even more impressive, for during the first 7 months of the program the crime in the four categories listed above fell by 17.62 percent. The other crime figures held steady so that we know that the police force was not merely shifting its efforts from one area of crime to another.

Now, looking at the basic question of the allocation of resources within a police department or within a municipality, we can look at one method in which such allocation might be altered. Right now in many cities and states of the Union, a person beaten up in the streets and left with permanent brain damage cannot sue for injuries. The attacker, if caught, will be jailed. That really does not help the victim, who ends up paying taxes for the prisoner's room and board!

If, on the other hand, the city or state were held liable for all damages sustained, the victim (or dependents) could sue the city or state for compensation. Unlimited liability on the part of government for crimes against the populace would certainly alter the present allocation of resources between crime prevention and other public endeavors. Under present laws the private cost of crime is borne by the individual, who has little hope of being compensated. It is true that some states now provide some liability, but it is certainly not enough. Right now, no state has to pay the full cost of crime against the public. Hence suboptimal expenditures for crime prevention and control now prevail.

We must be careful, though, to avoid what lawyers call

"moral hazard." If victims of robberies, for example, are fully compensated by the municipality, there will be less incentive for individuals to protect themselves privately against robberies. The same is true for other crimes. One way to avoid this is by establishing a deductible in the liability on the part of the municipality. In other words, it might be that the municipality is held responsible for all losses in excess of, say, $500 for home robberies. If this were the case, then homeowners would still have an incentive to lock their doors, have watchdogs, and keep lights on at night when they are away.

Crime costs. So does crime prevention. But the latter also has benefits to society which can be weighed in the making of decisions about law-enforcement methods and expenditures.

THE ECONOMICS OF CRIME AND PUNISHMENT

Is there a relationship between punishment and number and types of crimes committed? If so, what are the available alternatives to punishing guilty offenders? Should we allow large fines instead of incarceration? Should we have public whippings? Should capital punishment be allowed? In terms of establishing a system of crime deterrence, we might want to assess carefully the value of different methods of supposed deterrents.

One thing we can be sure of. Uniformity of heavy punishments for all crimes will lead to a larger number of major crimes being committed. Let's look at the reasoning. All decisions are made on the margin. If an act of theft will be punished by hanging and an act of murder will be punished by the same fate, there is no marginal deterrence to murder. If a theft of $5 is met with a punishment of ten years in jail and a theft of $50,000 also incurs a ten-year sentence, then why not steal $50,000? Why not go for broke? There is no marginal deterrence to prevent one from doing so.

A very serious question exists as to how our system of justice can establish penalties which are appropriate from a social point of view. To establish the correct (marginal) deterrents, we must observe empirically how criminals respond to changes in punishments. This leads us to the question of how people decide whether to commit a "crime." A theory needs to be established as to what determines the supply of criminal offenses.

Adam Smith once said:

The affluence of the rich excites the indignation of the poor, who are often both driven by want, and prompted by envy, to invade his possessions. It is only under the shelter of the civil magistrate that the owner of that valuable property, which is acquired by the labour of many years, or perhaps by many successive generations, can sleep a single night in security. He is at all times surrounded by unknown enemies, whom, though he never provokes, he can never appease, and from whose injustice he can be protected only by the powerful arm of the civil magistrate continually held up to chastise it. The acquisition of valuable and extensive property, therefore, necessarily requires the establishment of civil government. Where there is no property, or at least none that exceeds the value of two or three days' labour, civil government is not so necessary.[1]

Smith is pointing out that robberies involve the taking of valuable property. Thus, we can surmise that individuals who engage in robberies are seeking income. A professional criminal might be expected to look therefore at the expected returns and the expected costs of criminal activity. These could then be compared with the net returns from legitimate activities. We note that the civil government which Smith refers to in the above quote would be imposing the cost on the criminal if apprehended. That cost would include, but not be limited to, apprehension, conviction, and jail. (This is analogous to the cost that athletes may encounter when they get injured.)

Viewing the supply of offenses thusly, we can come up with methods by which society can lower the net expected rate of

[1] Adam Smith, *The Wealth of Nations*, 1776.

return for committing any illegal activity. That is, we can figure out how to reduce crime most effectively. We have talked about one particular aspect—the size of penalties. We also briefly mentioned the other—that is, the probability of detection for each offense. When either of these costs of crime goes up, the supply of offenses goes down; that is, less crime is committed.

Can this theory be applied to a decision pro or con on capital punishment? Sociologists, psychologists, and others have numerous theories correlating the number of murders committed to various psychological, sociological, and demographic variables. Some researchers believe that the higher the density of population, the more murders will be committed. Others contend that because we no longer have a nuclear family, there will be more murders committed. Economists consider these factors important, but not primary.

Now we start with a commodity called the act of murder. If the act of murder is like any other commodity, the quantity "demanded" (by perpetrators, of course, not victims) will be negatively related to the relative price. But what is the price of murder? Ignoring now all of the sociological, psychological, or psychic costs of murder, we have to consider the cost to the murderer when he or she is caught. Thus, we have to consider the probability of being caught, and then, once caught, the possible jail sentence or capital punishment that may be called for. But here again, we have to look at the probability of a particular jail sentence and the probability of going to the gas chamber, or the guillotine, or the four winds. Thus, it would do little good to observe the difference in murder rates between states that had capital punishment and states that did not. Rather, it would be necessary to look at the probability of a convicted murderer going to the gas chamber in those states that had capital punishment compared to what happened in states where there was a zero probability. In fact, there are some states with capital punishment where effectively the probability of going to the gas chamber is zero for a convicted murderer. We find, for example, that states with the death penalty for first-degree murder often change the charge to second-degree murder. But states with life maximums for first-degree murder give them more frequently.

Now, immediately critics of such analysis point to the "fact" that the murderer either in a moment of unreasoned passion or when confronted with an unanticipated situation during an armed robbery does not take into account the expected probability of going to the gas chamber. That is to say, murderers are not acting rationally when they murder. Is this a valid criticism of the economic model of the demand for murder? No, it is not. If the model predicts poorly, then the assumptions must be changed or the model changed in some other way. Indeed, if one contends that the expected "price" of committing a murder has no effect on the quantity of murders, one is implicitly negating the law of demand or stating that the price elasticity of the demand for murder is zero. One is also confusing the average murderer with the marginal murderer. All potential murderers do not have to be aware or react to the change in the expected "price" of committing a murder for the theory to be useful. If there are a sufficient number of marginal murderers who act as if they were responding to the higher expected "price" of murdering, then the demand curve for murders by perpetrators will be downward sloping.

A few economists have actually worked through economic models of the demand for murder and other crimes. One of the variables they put in was the objective conditional risk of execution—in other words, the risk of being executed if caught and convicted of murder. Two elasticities that were given in one study were —0.06 and —0.065.[2] While these elasticities are relatively small, they are not zero. The implication of these elasticities, given the number of murders and executions over the period of study in question, which was 1935 to 1969, was striking. The implied trade-off between murders and executions was between 7 and 8. "Put differently, an additional

[2] Isaac Erlich, "The Deterrent Effect of Capital Punishment: A Question of Life and Death," *The American Economic Review*, vol. 65, no. 3 (June 1973), p. 414.

execution per year over the period in question may have resulted, on average, in 7 or 8 fewer murders."[3] Similar evidence for felonies, such as burglary, robbery, etc., has also been compiled.[4]

One final note. In the case of capital punishment, the execution must be thought to fall on the guilty parties, rather than randomly applied. History tells us that under the emperors in China, executions were frequent. However, the emperors were not always quite so good at getting the right person. This system of "punishment" does little good for society in terms of combatting crime, not to mention the loss suffered by the innocent victim and his or her family due to perverted justice.

[3] *Ibid.*, p. 414.
[4] See, for example, Arleen Smigel, "Does Crime Pay? An Economic Analysis," Unpublished M.A. thesis, Columbia University, 1965.

THE ECONOMICS OF
BRIBERY

The following is a tale of bribery that many New Yorkers and indeed Chicagoans, San Franciscans, Pittsburghers, and other cities' residents are familiar with. Mr. X, a Manhattan business consultant, moves his office from a midtown building to an East Side apartment house. Several days before moving day, a telephone company installer calls him up and asks him to come down right away. Mr. X does so. The installer informs him that he cannot get to the installation for a couple of weeks. Mr. X gives him $10, and the telephones are installed immediately. Apparently that was just a beginning.

The next night Mr. X moves four large cartons of books and related items from his midtown office to his new East Side apartment. But the night custodian does not let Mr. X through the large, nonrevolving doors. However, $5 gets them quickly unlocked. Unfortunately, the super comes down at the same time, and another $5 must be meted out.

Then arrival at the new office: A $20 "gratuity" is asked by the new super. When a few minor repairs are needed for the new office, the super must be given $25 more.

This tale of surreptitious and not-so-surreptitious payoffs or bribes to individuals in positions of economic power is a way of life for many residents in large cities. Moreover, the bribes are certainly not limited to private individuals working for private organizations. In fact, one could surmise that bribery is more a way of life when dealing with officials, working in an official capacity. Certainly the Knapp Commission discovered widespread bribery within the New York City police department. Similar commissions have discovered similar situations of overt payoffs to police officials by private citizens wishing to engage in activities that were either illegal or allowable only after a payoff to an official (even if they were, strictly speaking, not against the law).

And to be sure, bribery is not restricted to large cities in the United States. In fact, it is much more a way of life in certain less developed countries. There are even firms that specialize in bribery in India, where the bureaucratic red tape for doing just about anything is a mile long. A colleague of ours counted no fewer than eighty-seven signatures on his application for an exit visa from that country. In Mexico and other Latin American countries *la mordida* (the little bite) is a necessary cost of doing business or of mere day-to-day living.

Let's try to apply some economic principles to figure out why bribery exists, where we would expect to find it most frequently, and how it might be reduced.

First of all we define bribery as a payment over and above any legally specified payment for obtaining a good or a service. This puts into the bribery category all "gratuities" to individuals in official capacities who must rule on the legality of private citizens' actions. Hence we call a bribe any payment to a city housing inspector, for example, for an okay to complete a house without having to go through additional red tape in order to get a building permit. We also count as a bribe a payment to a policeperson so as to double-park while delivering supplies to a customer. Obviously, individuals will offer bribes whenever the benefit exceeds the cost of the bribe. In cases where there is a zero chance of being harmed by attempting to bribe an official, each individual would be willing to make a bribe up to the point where the bribe just equals the benefits received. As an example, a person attempting to get a permit for a building addition might be willing to bribe a building inspector with $1000 if the value to that individual of obtaining the permit immediately was at least worth $1000, rather than wading through the normal red tape and waiting period, and rather than paying lawyers' costs and hearing fees for the permit. Obviously a bribe is only appropriate in a situation of this nature, in which laws exist preventing unrestricted economic activity. If there were no law regulating the construction of additional structures on existing property, there would be no official issuing the permit and there would be no room for bribery.

We therefore find that some of the most frequent occasions of bribery are in the area of economic regulations that restrict economic activity on the part of individuals or businesses. This will be true, for example, with respect to all activities involving illegal goods such as drugs. But it extends to all restrictions on just about any type of economic activity. Restrictions prohibiting the number of taxicabs is one case in which officials charged with enforcing that restriction could be open to bribes by gypsy cab owners. Restrictions on working during Sundays is another area where bribery might be evident. Those individuals and businesses who wish to violate the law and work on Sunday would be willing to pay officials charged with enforcing the no-work law up to the extent that the benefits from working just equaled the bribery that was necessary in order to be able to work on Sunday.

Of course there are other politically inspired situations that are also open to bribery. The letting of public contracts for the construction of roads, buildings, and so on, has often created a situation conducive to bribery of public officials: Witness the reasons behind the forced resignation of former Vice-President Spiro Agnew. He was accused (though not convicted) of accepting bribes or payoffs from large construction company executives in his home state while governor, presumably in exchange for lucrative (i.e., highly profitable) construction contracts.

Indeed, it turns out that most bribery scandals seem to involve government bureaucrats or officials. A few years ago when the tremendous Lockheed Aircraft payments to foreign officials were uncovered, many Americans were shocked. While it is impossible for an economist to pass moral judgment on such business activities, we can point out that virtually all of the companies accused of engaging in illegal bribery abroad were dealing directly with government officials who had control over important business contracts, such as the purchase of millions of dollars' worth of airplanes. It appears that in order to do at least some types of business abroad, firms must be willing to consider, as part of their costs, bribes to foreign officials in charge of letting large contracts. If, indeed, the U.S. government were effective in preventing American companies from competing in this manner, presumably companies in other countries would be able to get more business by continuing to engage in payoffs. Actually, when a U.S. company gives a bribe to a foreign official in order to obtain a license, right to deal, large contract, or any other "favor," this action is no different than a U.S. company giving Christmas presents to its best domestic customers.

In a highly politicized living environment where numerous rules and regulations govern the day-to-day lives of individuals and businesses, it has been argued that, although bribery is rampant—such as outlined above when we referred to the New York City police department, its existence allows for the more efficient allocation of resources within the constrained environment. What could possibly be meant here? To find out, all we have to do is ask ourselves what the effect of a bribe is on the allocation of resources. It has the same effect that the legal payment of the going price for just about anything in the private sector has. It causes resources to gravitate to where they have the highest value to consumers. If, for example, consumers find that they can never get a taxicab when they need one and some owners of four-door sedans are willing to provide taxicab services, the payment of a bribe to the appropriate officials so that those gypsies can operate will benefit the owners of the cabs and consumers alike. Rather than the sedans being used in a less valuable activity, they are used in a more valuable one. However, note that this is only true when there are not significant externalities present and private and social returns diverge. In such cases, bribery can work in the exactly reverse direction, as for example when a well-known pickpocket bribes a security guard in a public or private gathering place such as in a hotel lobby or an airport.

A useful way of looking at bribery is that it is a tax on producers and/or consumers. Again, you might ask, how can that be? Consider the following example. If, in order to double-park three times a week in front of a restaurant in order to unload supplies, the supplier must pay the local beat police officer a bribe, that becomes an increased cost of doing business. The supplier ultimately will include that increased cost in the price of restaurant supplies. The restauranteur will ultimately include that higher supply price in the price charged you and me to eat in the restaurant. The police officer, on the other hand, receives the bribe as a form of income. In a competitive situation, police officers' salaries will be lower by the amount of the average bribe taken in. Hence, rather than paying higher taxes to pay higher wages, we pay lower taxes. The police officers receive increased compensation in the form of bribes, and we pay a higher price for restaurant food to account for those bribes.

We now turn to the question of how society could improve the level of enforcement of its laws, that is, reduce the amount of bribery and therefore illegal activity, assuming that is what society wants to do. We know that an enforcer, be he a police officer, building inspector, or what have you, will not accept a bribe if the gain from enforcing the law exceeds that bribe. Therefore, whenever the gain from enforcement is less than the potential bribe (i.e., the loss from punishment to violators of the law in question), bribery, intimidation, and harassment will ensue. Another way of looking at this is in the negative. What is the loss that could be sustained by an enforcer, such as a police officer or a building inspector, if the acceptance of a bribe were discovered? In general, the only loss due to discovery is the loss of his job. If the bribee, as it were, is not making wages in excess of what he could receive in other types of occupations, then there is little incentive to worry about being caught, for a similarly paying job presumably can be substituted for the one just lost.

This leads us to an interesting proposition. We could improve enforcement of laws by paying enforcers higher than prevailing wages, not because higher wages would attract more public-spirited, honest citizens, but rather because those higher wages would make the opportunity cost of being caught accepting a bribe relatively high. Hence there would be fewer bribes accepted.

Another alternative method of reducing the amount of bribery is to reduce the number of laws and regulations that either limit or restrict what some consider to be normal competitive economic activity and to reduce or eliminate laws regulating crimes that have no victims. As economists, we cannot suggest that these latter two courses of action are either appropriate or desirable. We can only point out the implications in terms of a predicted reduction in bribery and hence illegal activity.

2

THE ECONOMICS OF
PUBLIC
HIGHER EDUCATION

In modern times we have come to recognize that investment in human beings contributes as much to economic growth as does investment in capital equipment. Because property rights are effective and enforced we do not need to worry about investment in new plant and equipment. The private profitability of such investment ensures that interest rates will be "high" enough to attract suppliers of loanable funds into that market.[1] But what about the human-capital market? To operate our complicated technical equipment and the resulting complex organizational structure, we need highly trained and educated engineers, scientists, doctors, and lawyers. If one form of capital is scarce relative to the other, the scarcer form normally commands a higher price. This situation will induce suppliers of loanable funds to invest in that form of capital. For example, if the interest rate on a loan to build a factory is 10 percent, but there is a dearth of skilled engineers to operate the factory, the price of engineers will rise. Accordingly, the rate of return on becoming an engineer (reflected in the present net value of his discounted earnings stream) will rise. In effect, the rate of return on investing in an engineer would rise to, say, 20 percent.

[1] Assuming no problems of externality exist.

Other things being equal, we would expect suppliers of funds to shift from the physical-capital market to the human-capital market until the supply schedule of funds in the latter has increased so much that the quantity of engineers is sufficient to make the expected rate of return in both markets equal (an additional dollar invested in either market produces the same rate of return). But then, other things are *not* equal!

It is not that the rate of return on human-capital investment has not been high. Historically, it has paid to go to college; this payment is reflected in the lifetime-earnings stream of different educational levels. However, it is one thing for an entrepreneur to go to a bank, present his qualifications, and borrow money for a capital investment. It is something else when a student presents his academic credentials and asks to borrow the funds for a college education. The former can pledge the plant as collateral; the latter cannot offer equal security.[2] Accordingly, bankers and other suppliers of funds have not been able to practice *arbitrage* (equating the rates of return by shifting funds from one market to another) in the market, since the security and risks cannot be equated because of the nature of property rights. As one would expect under these circumstances, there has been a tendency in many countries to underinvest in human beings.

It is probably true that the United States underinvested in human beings in earlier periods as well. But it is not evident today. In fact, it is possible that we are investing too much. How has an imperfect market for human beings that was characterized by underinvestment turned into one that may be characterized by overinvestment?

Suppose we first review what constitutes the "right" amount. The correct amount of higher education is one at which the social return on the investment in human capital is equal at the margin to other types of social investment (i.e., the opportunity costs of capital are equated at the margin). The social costs of higher education are (a) the direct costs—that is, tui-

[2] Note, however, that students admitted to medical school can borrow large sums of money from banks. Why? Because most medical students become doctors and earn high and steady incomes. And, it is very easy to keep track of doctors in order to make sure that they pay off their loans.

tion, room, board, books; (b) an additional subsidy, in the case of public universities, which is provided by the state from tax revenues; and (c) the income forgone by the student while in college—that is, his or her opportunity costs during the student years. The social benefits are (a) the lifetime incremental earnings yielded the student by four years of college—that is, the difference between the earnings that would have been received during a lifetime as a high-school graduate and the earnings that will be received as a college graduate; (b) the consumption value of higher education—that is, the value of an education for aesthetic enjoyment of books, art, music, etc.; (c) any external benefits that society receives from a better-educated citizenry. Both the costs and the benefits should be discounted back to the present to make them comparable.

Recent studies have been made on the returns to higher education, and they indicate that the rate of return in real terms and adjusted for the influence of ability and family background ranges from 11 percent for those with some college but no degree to about 2 percent for those with a Ph.D. degree. Similar social rates of return for those with an undergraduate degree are about 8 percent on the average. In contrast, private rates of return range from 15 percent for those with some college but not degree to about 4 percent for those with a Ph.D. They are about 11 percent for those with an undergraduate degree.[3] These rates of return are significantly lower than the rates of return on physical-capital investments; that is, the social rates of return are lower. Calculations excluding the consumption return and possible external benefits have been made in various studies, and these show a rate of return of 10 to 15 percent.

There is no reason to expect that the opportunity costs of higher education will necessarily tend to be equated at the margin. To see why, let's look at colleges and universities from

[3] F. Thomas Juster (ed.), *Education, Income and Human Behavior: A Report Prepared for the Carnegie Commission on Higher Education and the National Bureau on Economic Research* (New York: McGraw-Hill, 1975), p. 14.

three different viewpoints—those of the student, of the parent, and of the state legislature. We will observe that each considers different parts of the total social costs and benefits in making the calculations.

The cost to students is the income forgone during college plus whatever percentage of other college expenses they pay themselves as distinguished from those paid by their parents. Children from poorer families tend to have to work their way through college and to shoulder a larger share of the direct costs. The benefits are the consumption benefits plus the increased lifetime-income stream. The lifetime earnings of a typical college graduate are about $185,000 more than those of a high-school graduate. The student pays only a portion, and usually a very small portion, of the costs, and receives all the consumption and investment benefits. It would clearly be worth his or her while to go to college, even if the social rate of return on college had fallen below the social equilibrium rate.

The parents, typically, bear the major share of the direct costs of a college education plus a minuscule fraction of the state subsidy as taxpayers. Costs approximate $3320 per year for a state college for fees, books, room and board, etc. The benefits are vicarious. Parents enjoy watching the consumption and investment returns of their offspring and derive some prestige from boasting about their children's graduation from college. Just what the equilibrium rate of investment for parents may be would be difficult to measure, but it is clearly not the same as for either students or legislators.

Legislators appropriate an amount of money each year to make up the difference between the tuition (plus any other income the university may receive) and the total costs of operating the university.[4] Grants from the federal government, endowments, foundations, and gifts provide additional funds. The rest of it must come from appropriations by the legislature. In the state of Washington, appropriations for all the in-

[4] For the University of Washington, as a more or less typical example, the tuition is $564 per person; totaled for all students this payment accounts for approximately 10 percent of the university's budget.

stitutions of higher learning (beyond the twelfth grade) for the 1974–1976 biennium involved an expenditure by the state of approximately $1 billion; this was 18.5 percent of the total budget and equal to $150 in tax monies for every man, woman, and child in the state.

Why do states subsidize higher education, and what determines the amount? Partly, they are influenced by parents of college students who form a potent political group and are receiving a subsidy from other taxpayers. Those who are subsidized obviously wish to perpetuate the system. Partly, the influence is the American heritage that education is a right (like free parks) that everyone should enjoy regardless of income. And partly it is that there is a widespread view that external benefits are associated with a more educated society. significant external benefits are associated with a more educated society.

The first contention is a matter of political survival and is hard to argue down, although it is probably the single most important cause of the continued high level of spending on higher education. The second contention implies that all who wish to do so should be able to go to college. This could become more of a reality if the market for human capital were perfected, perhaps by more government loans to students. The third contention may provide another clue to continued legislative support. It is widely contended that a better-educated society has less crime, less juvenile delinquency, etc., and that a higher proportion of college-educated adults in a state makes for a better society. How much truth this view contains is hard to say. Certainly, in recent years legislators have been shaken in their faith in a college education, and have come to perceive some external diseconomies to counter the alleged external economies.[5] Note, though, that such side effects are supposedly

[5] We should note that we have ignored two additional considerations which influence appropriations. The state legislature is concerned with benefits within the state—not with the general social welfare. This should tend to induce the legislator to raise out-of-state tuition, but it also means he or she cannot capture any benefits from graduates who move away.

a function of *all* higher education, whether in the form of engineering training or liberal-arts training.

Most technical higher education involves very specific training, presumably useful to the student in a limited area of job pursuits. Technical students reap the benefits (obtain a rate of return) from their specialized training. Their employers have to pay them the value of their marginal product and so do not usually, in a competitive labor market, obtain excess returns from the skills of specialized students. Therefore, it is not obvious that *government* should be subsidizing that part of schooling which is technical in nature.

The positive externalities—a more informed citizenry, less crime, etc.—appear historically to have come from *general* education, which requires fewer resources than does technical education. Unless it can be shown that technical education also generates positive externalities, there may be no valid argument for its subsidization.

Certainly in the latter part of the 1970s, many taxpayers and policymakers are wondering why it is advisable to continue high levels of subsidization to colleges and universities which don't seem to be teaching very much anymore. Employers can no longer look upon high university or college grades as clear evidence of superior ability. Grade inflation has been rampant throughout the latter part of this decade. In a recent ten-year period, the University of North Carolina doubled the percentage of A's that it handed out. A few years ago, more than eighty percent of the graduating class at Harvard College obtained degrees *cum laude*. In a ten-year period at the University of Wisconsin, the average grade increased from a C+ to a B+. We certainly can't explain grade inflation in terms of students knowing more by the time they get to college. Student

---

Moreover, the legislator may recognize another side benefit (externality) from a university which is probably of substantial magnitude—that is, advances in knowledge from research. Again, however, most of the benefits from research redound to society as a whole, although some, such as agricultural research, may be specific to state problems and tend accordingly to be handsomely supported.

achievement test scores (SATs) and National Merit Examination Scores given to graduating high school seniors have shown dramatic *drops* in the last decade.

How can we explain what has happened? A little supply and demand analysis might help. The demand for higher education has not been growing at the rapid pace that was customary through the late 1950s and all of the 1960s. The number of potential college students has diminished due to changes in population trends, and a college diploma has become much more common; its prestige value is not as great as it used to be. On the supply side, however, just the opposite had occurred during all of this period. State institutions increased the number of buildings and dormitories dramatically in the 1960s and we have seen a tremendous upsurge in the number of community and technical colleges throughout the country. The result has been a greater shift in the supply of higher education than in the demand. The implicit price has had to fall. One part of the implicit price that students pay when they go to college is the amount of work they are expected to undertake in order to get a given grade. Academic standards, as it were, have fallen in response to the new supply and demand conditions in higher education. So, we have seen not only general grade inflation, but also a reduction in the number of required general education courses, and a loosening of social regulations.

It remains to be seen whether this trend will continue. There are some students who are demanding a return to higher academic standards so that when they go out into the job market, their degree and their grade-point average will generate useful information to potential employers. After all, grade inflation actually hurts the truly superior student who must now devise alternative means of signalling potential employers that he or she is truly better than all the other A students from the same university.

28

THE ECONOMICS OF LOWER EDUCATION

The public school system is in trouble. School levies are being challenged everywhere, and frequently are voted down. The tax basis of schools is not only considered unfair but is being successfully fought in the courts as favoring the rich over the poor (and in a few cases, vice versa). Teachers are going on strike with increasing frequency. And schoolchildren continue to be bored silly by the system. As further evidence that the public school system doesn't seem to be fulfilling parents' and students' expectations, we note that even though the school-age population is now declining, enrollments in private schools have been increasing steadily since 1974. No longer the bastion of children from rich families, an increasingly large number of students come from middle class homes, in spite of the stiff $2000–$5000 annual cost of private schools. Not all of this general malaise with public schools lends itself to economic analysis, but a surprising amount of it does.

Lower education, like public higher education, is paid for by taxes, but it differs from the latter in that attendance is compulsory. Education through twelfth grade is mandatory in most states, and in all states it is provided by tax-financed institutions. There is very little choice involved in the sense that taxes must be paid, usually in the form of a levy on the value of real property, whether or not a person has school-age children and whether or not a parent desires to send his or her child to a public institution. Wealthier parents do have options, but they are severely limited. Private grade schools, junior highs, and high schools do exist, but there aren't very many. And the reason is easy to see. Since all parents have to pay for education through property taxes, many do not feel they can afford more or that the additional value they receive from sending their children to private school is worth the extra cost. Parents who do send their children to private schools end up paying twice, in effect, once through property taxes and once to the private institution. These parents must consider the value of a private school education to exceed substantially the value of education that would be received in the local public school.

Poorer parents who are not very mobile have literally no choice in terms of how their younger children should be educated. Parents who are able to move to a different area in order to be able to send their children to a different school can have more say. In fact, the quality of education offered varies tremendously from school district to school district and even from one school to another. Although not a primary determinant, an important element is the amount of money spent per pupil. This amount varies greatly from incredibly low figures in Southern rural areas and some ghettos to very high figures in Scarsdale, New York, and other posh suburbs. Parents therefore can have a choice in the quality of schooling their children will receive, even without sending them to private schools, but only if they are willing to move to an area where they feel the schools are better. The quality of schools is a strong selling point for some suburban areas. You need only drive around with a real-estate agent in Scarsdale or Beverly Hills or Palo Alto or numerous other communities where the public schools are considered above average. The real-estate agent will certainly let you know.

One of the major reasons for the disparity in the amount of money spent per pupil in different areas of the country is the manner in which funds for public education are raised. In almost all cases, it is property taxes that are used to finance public education at the lower levels. The yield of property taxes is a function not only of the rate of taxation but also of the base to which this rate is applied. In a very poor area with low housing values, the base is relatively small. This is not the case in wealthier suburban areas. It is not surprising, therefore, to find $500 per pupil per year spent in a ghetto and $1800 per pupil per year spent in the suburbs.

A few years ago, several court cases were brought by children (with the aid of their parents) against school districts that were spending less per pupil than other districts. The suits, claiming discrimination due to location, were won in lower-court decisions. It appeared that many districts would have to alter the methods by which they financed their schools in order to equalize better the per-pupil expenditures throughout districts, states, and even the nation. If the equalization were to be achieved by improvement in the quality of education in poorer areas, it would necessarily mean that more money would have to be spent on education in general. After all, it is usually difficult to improve the quality of something without spending more money, although we shall have cause to question this generalization below. The Supreme Court reversed at least one of the lower-court decisions so that it is not clear what effect all of these court cases will have on school financing.

In the meantime, nonpublic schools have run into extreme financial problems. Enrollment in the past 10 years has declined by almost 25 percent. At least part of this decline is due to increases in the tuition that parents must pay in order to send their children to private schools. The rest is best explained by declining birth rates, especially among Catholics, who account for more than 80 percent of the enrollment in nonpublic schools. Additionally, there has been a shift of the population to the suburbs, where public schools seem to satisfy parents more than they do in urban areas. And, finally, there has been an apparent decline in interest in religious education.

The major variable expense in a school budget is the teachers' salaries. In order to meet teachers' demands for higher salaries, special levies and extraordinary state appropriations are necessary. This dependency leads teachers to have a direct interest in politics. Schoolteachers are numerous. They vote, they are articulate, and each one has a captive audience. We have come to observe that a "passionate" minority whose vote for a legislator will be determined by a single issue has more power than the average voters who will be influenced by a large number of issues. The legislator will lose all of the votes of the first group if he or she does not agree with the issue but can expect to receive his or her "share" of the average voters' votes even though the average voter may disagree with some of his or her positions. It's not hard to see why schoolteachers have become one of the most powerful state political lobbies.

Recently, teachers themselves have faced discontent from two directions—disgruntled taxpayers and disenchanted children. It should be evident from the foregoing discussion why taxpayers are disgruntled. If they have no school-age children, they are subsidizing those who do; if they are well-to-do parents and do not like the quality of public education, they must pay twice to send their children to private schools; if they are poor parents, they have little choice at all. Moreover, there is a growing dissatisfaction with the quality of lower education even where per-pupil expenditures are high. On the face of it, this is not surprising to an economist. We do not have a good way to measure educational output (i.e., what we are producing with teaching and other educational inputs), and there are few incentives to encourage teachers to innovate or improve performance (whatever the measure of output). What taxpayers do see is that each year the school is costing them more, and they can see little evidence that the product (however it is measured) is better. Their reaction is to oppose increased school expenditures. The disenchantment of schoolchildren is carried over at least partly from their parents and partly from living in a world where information costs have fallen dramatically (i.e., they are more knowledgeable at an earlier age). A lot of this disenchantment goes beyond economic analysis. Violence has become a terrifying fact of life in many schools. Between frozen salaries and recalcitrant kids, a public school teacher's lot is often not a happy one.

Lower education is a world of nonmarket decision-making, and the malaise we have described is another way of saying that the various groups—taxpayers, parents, teachers, and schoolchildren—are frustrated. But why should this be so? Public school education grew up and largely replaced the private school in the nineteenth century because citizens believed: (a) that there were positive externalities associated with an educated populace; and (b) that equality of opportunity was a right that could be guaranteed only by such a system. Public-supported education had the overwhelming approval of the citizenry. It is doubtful that most Americans have changed their minds. But can we preserve these objectives and still resolve the problems that are frustrating us? The problem is one that is becoming ever more important as more and more economic decisions are made outside the marketplace. The process of nonmarket decision-making was examined in more detail in the last chapter. The issues are the same: How do we develop responsive institutional arrangements when we do not resort to the market mechanism?

One alternative currently under consideration is the use of educational vouchers. With this system, the laws requiring school attendance are kept, but parents are not required to send their children to public schools. Rather, each set of parents is given an educational voucher that can be used in any educational institution appropriate for their children. Parents will then send their children to the institutions they prefer. Some parents will spend more than the educational voucher provides, just as some parents send their children to private school while still paying property taxes that go to support public schools. This does not mean that public educational institutions will not exist. All that it will mean is that public schools will have to compete with private schools, which will enter the market in offering services to parents, because parents will now have the wherewithal to make a choice. There would not be discrimination against people because they have to live in ghettos where property taxes yield relatively small amounts of taxes. Discrimination in the sense of unequal expenditures for different pupils will be eliminated. An experiment was started in 1972 in which educational vouchers could be used by several thousand parents in San Jose, California. The vouchers were not usable in private schools, however; they were to be used only in four or five public schools in a certain area. The results of this experiment will therefore be of limited value. It is only when the private market is allowed to come into play that we can tell whether or not a system of educational vouchers will actually work. It is highly controversial. It would introduce competition into the lower educational system; give parents more choice about their children's education; threaten the tenure system of teachers (poor or unpopular teachers would not get students, and their schools would either fire them or go out of business); and significantly alter the distribution of the tax burden. But whether or not we view these results as good or bad depends on how we measure the consequences of educational competition, greater parental choice, and undermining the tenure system, and on how the tax burden is redistributed. Once we have that information, our values may cause us to disagree about the desirability of the consequences. But we must first get the facts.

THE ECONOMICS OF
PERSONAL INCOME
DISTRIBUTION

Can we make sense out of Dr. J's shift from the New York Nets to the Philadelphia 76ers for a reported $600,000 a year, 6 year contract? What about the 1975 contract received by drivers of garbage trucks in Seattle for an annual salary in excess of $17,000 for a 35-hour week? Is there any rationale that will explain Nelson Rockefeller's income at the same time that it can explain that of a migrant worker in California's central valley?

Well to start with, more than three quarters of total national income is labor income, so that any explanation must try to make sense out of differentials received for payments to labor. Here recent research has begun to make a significant dent in our ignorance. Specifically, a recent study by Jacob Mincer shows that we can account for more than 70 percent of the differential incomes of white urban males as a result of the differences in the distribution of investments in human capital. This includes not only the formal schooling that people receive, which explains about one-fourth of the differences in income, but, in addition, postschooling investments, that is, on-the-job training accounts for another fourth, that is, on-the-job training and skills acquired in the course of a job itself. Differential schooling costs for a given number of years and systematic differences in hours worked attributable to human capital account for the additional amounts.[1]

When we go beyond schooling to explore the remaining differentials, these are attributable to inherited wealth, differential in innate ability and intelligence, individual taste, economic rents, exploitation and discrimination, monopoly, and finally good luck. The first two of these need little additional explanation. Inherited wealth and intelligence are attributes that will provide returns to those with the good fortune to have received them. Individual taste requires more explanation. Some people may prefer leisure to work and simply may not be willing to work very hard. Other people may be risk preferrers rather than risk averters, a subject we have discussed in Chapter 13. Suffice it to note at this point that a risk preferrer may be willing, at very high odds, to attempt to undertake some activity in which the payoff would be very big if he succeeds but in which he will fall flat on his face and receive no return if he fails. Thus someone could decide to become a professional basketball player, but the odds of becoming a Dr. J. are very small, indeed. And, in fact, the example of Dr. J. illustrates the next point about economic rents, because he has a unique talent that cannot be duplicated by others. As a result, because of this unique talent, he can earn an income substantially higher than that of other basketball players or indeed most other individuals. Take the Beatles, for another example; as an incipient rock group in Liverpool, they made small incomes, much smaller than they could have made at that time as taxi drivers. They opted for a low income with a small chance of eventually making a very large one. Once their specialized talents were discovered and promoted, they obtained that very large income. In fact, they obtained an income far exceeding what was needed to induce them to keep

[1] Jacob Mincer, "Education, Experience and the Distribution of Earnings and Employment: An Overview," in F. Thomas Juster (ed.), *Education, Income and Human Behavior* (New York: McGraw-Hill, 1975).

singing. Economists say that this extra income represents economic rent earned by their remarkably specialized resources. The same analysis holds for the Rolling Stones, Tom Jones, Frank Sinatra, Bob Dylan, Glenn Gould, Leontyne Price, Jane Fonda, John Galbraith, Milton Friedman, Paul Samuelson, and Raquel Welch. They are all collecting economic rents, income over and above the amount that would induce them to continue in their present occupations.

Exploitation and discrimination also affect the distribution of income. Even with equal educational achievement, both in quality and quantity, certain groups may not, and actually do not, receive incomes equal to those of other groups. This is a subject we will treat in the next chapter.

How about monopoly power? If any group of sellers of a service or a product can create a monopoly, that group predictably will earn monopoly returns, if they can exclude others from entering that particular industry. That happens to fit our example of the Seattle garbage-truck drivers. Historically, it also fits the American Medical Association.

And finally we are left with good luck. It is not just winning the Irish Sweepstakes or getting the winning ticket from the New York State lottery. It is simply being in the right place at the right time when things break for you. Luck, good or bad, surely is an important factor. But then, as we said in Chapter 11, "Risk and Insurance," that is what the game is all about.

THE ECONOMICS OF
EXPLOITATION
AND
DISCRIMINATION

Urban nonwhite males are estimated to have earned more than 36 percent less than urban white males in 1975.

Blacks obtain lower rates of return on the average from investing in a college education than do whites.

Ghetto dwellers pay more on the average for equal quality in housing, food, and clothing, than do nonghetto residents.

Do the above facts confirm that exploitation and discrimination exist? Before answering this question, we need to examine the economic connotations of these two explosive words.

The everyday meaning of exploitation is simply not being paid enough for what you sell (labor services or goods) and having to pay too much for what you buy. Discrimination is usually taken to mean about the same as exploitation, but may also include not being able to find work at all and not being able to buy a certain product, such as housing in particular neighborhoods.

The economist's definition of *exploitation* is somewhat more restrictive. We consider in this book that a person is being exploited in the selling of his labor services if he is being paid less than the value of his marginal product. He is being exploited in the buying of goods and services if he pays a price that exceeds the (marginal) cost of the product or service he is buying. (Note here that "cost" also includes normal profits.)

Using the above definition of exploitation, let's see how it is possible for this phenomenon to exist. First and foremost, lack of information allows exploitation. When employees are ignorant of better job opportunities, they may be exploited by employers. When consumers are unaware of other and cheaper product sources, they may be exploited by sellers.

Restricted entry is another cause of exploitation. When a professional sports league prevents the entry of competing leagues, players may be exploited because of the monopsony power of the single existing major league employer, as described in Chapter 16. If a food merchant in an isolated town successfully prevents entry by new firms, consumers can be forced to pay monopoly rents over and above the competitive price of food.

Restricted mobility is another cause of exploitation. If, for example, lawyers are prevented from practicing in states other than the one where they now work, they may be exploited because they are not allowed to go where the value of their services (and their potential incomes) is highest.[1]

It should be noted that each of the last three paragraphs included the phrase "*may* be exploited." Stress is placed on the "may." The lack of information, of free entry, and of mobility does not *prima facie* indicate exploitation. More is needed. In terms of information, *all* employees or consumers concerned must be unaware of the facts—not just the average employee or consumer. For example, non-English-speaking immigrants arriving in America could be exploited only when they first set foot on shore (and even then not for long), for there were brokers who specialized in providing them with translated information. Competition among immigrant brokers assured that non-English-speaking employees received wages equal to the

---

[1] See letter to the Editor, *Ramparts* (August 1970).

value of their marginal product.[2] The point here is that information need not be obtained directly by the employee himself, since competition among employers will provide sufficient information (at the margin) to ensure nonexploitation. The same argument applies to the relation between consumers and sellers.

Nor is the mere lack of free entry enough to open the way for exploitation; those participating in the restricted side of the market must also agree among themselves not to compete against one another. Take, for example, the National Football League of 10 years ago. It restricted entry and *also,* via the "draft" system, prevented teams from bidding against each other. Otherwise, incentives for individual teams to compete for the best players normally would have netted players incomes equal to the value of their marginal products.

In general, then, exploitation requires restrictions on information, entry, and mobility plus additional arrangements to ensure that such restrictions affect *all* employees and consumers. Up to now we have been considering mainly the labor market. We now turn to product markets.

Ghetto consumers are known to pay higher prices for almost everything they buy. This is a true form of exploitation only if it can be demonstrated that the costs of providing products are no higher in ghettos than elsewhere. The evidence suggests that they are higher, because of: (a) relatively higher property insurance rates for ghetto businesses, (b) relatively higher "shrinkage" (theft) rates for ghetto stores, (c) relatively higher rates of violent crime in ghettos, and (d) relatively higher nonpayment for time purchases by ghetto residents.

It is true that the markup on ghetto-store products is higher than elsewhere, and that this tends to make for relatively higher net dollar profits on sales for ghetto merchants. But, after all the costs and taxes are taken out of these profits, the percentage rate of net return for ghetto retailers on the money

---

[2] This was on average lower than for the native-born, because the ability to use English increased productivity.

they have invested is lower than for general-market retailers.[3]

Exploitation as defined above may or may not exist in the ghetto; but there can be little doubt that *discrimination* does in fact exist or, as some economists euphemistically put it, that there are "tastes for discrimination" in our society.

We say that an employer has a taste for discrimination when he or she acts as if there were nonmoney costs associated with hiring blacks or other minority-group members. This behavior leads to lower incomes for blacks than they would receive otherwise.[4]

In a theoretical and empirical study of discrimination against blacks, Professor G. S. Becker[5] found that discrimination: (a) is positively related to the relative numbers of blacks and whites, and further is more prevalent when large numbers are involved in nonmarket actions, such as the attainment of formal education; (b) is less for those seeking temporary as opposed to permanent work; (c) is greater for those who are older and better educated; and (d) has deterred some blacks considering entering a profession from trying to enter law because of their competitive disadvantage in arguing before white juries.

One of Dr. Becker's empirical conclusions was that "[black] incomes would increase by 16 percent if market discrimination ceased."[6]

Discrimination against blacks has in a very real sense prevented them from acquiring as much human capital as whites. Even if blacks attend school as long, their scholastic achievement is less, for they typically are allotted more meager school

[3] Frederick D. Sturdivant (ed.), *The Ghetto Marketplace* (New York: The Free Press, 1969), p. 15.
[4] We defined exploitation as not receiving the value of one's marginal product. If we include the employer's psychic negative valuation of employing blacks, then discrimination does not imply exploitation; however, both result in lower incomes for those adversely affected.
[5] G. S. Becker, *The Economics of Discrimination*, 2nd ed. (Chicago: University of Chicago Press, 1971).
[6] *Ibid.*, p. 21.

resources than their white counterparts. Data from the 1960 census revealed that a large portion of the white/nonwhite income differential results from differences in both the quantity of education received and scholastic achievement (which is a function *inter alia* of the quality of education received). "Differences between whites and nonwhites in these two education-related factors are estimated to have accounted for nonwhite urban males receiving between 23 and 27 percent less income than white urban males in 1959. The size of these estimates indicates that unless differences between the two populations in these two factors can be reduced substantially, the median income of nonwhite males is unlikely to increase to more than 70 to 80 percent of that of whites, *even if employment discrimination is substantially reduced* [emphasis added]."[7]

Black (and certain other minority groups) are suffering from, among other things, too small investment in their human capital. But even when we take account of differences in quantity of education received, scholastic achievement, and regional, age, and city-size distributions (all factors which affect productivity), there remains an unexplained differential in income between blacks and whites of 14 to 25 percent for nonfarm occupations.[8] We are left with the inevitable conclusion that this difference is due to discrimination.

We note, though, that a detailed examination of the 1970 census has revealed that the relative economic status of minority groups improved during the 1960s. For example, the nonwhite/white median earnings ratio for males age 25–64 increased almost 17½ percent during that decade. This increase came from two sources: (1) nonwhite males faced improved employment opportunities and apparently "a decline in employment discrimination against blacks."[8] and (2) a large

[7] James Gwartney, "Discrimination and Income Differentials," *American Economic Review*, vol. 50, no. 3 (June 1970), p. 397.

[8] J. G. Haworth, James Gwartney, and C. Haworth, "Earnings, Productivity, and Changes in Employment Discrimination During the 1960s," *The American Economic Review*, vol. 65, no. 1 (March 1976), p. 67.

number of older nonwhite workers with low productivity and, hence, low relative earnings left the labor force to be replaced by younger, better-prepared nonwhites with higher relative earnings. It turned out that the improvement in relative earnings capacity was greatest for those nonwhites with the most education. The authors of the study from which these data were taken conclude that "progress was made during the 1960s toward breaking the cycle of poverty resulting from discriminatory employment practices."[9]

Discrimination as measured by differences in relative median money income of white and black families has, however, not improved in the 1970s. According to U.S. Census Bureau data, the relative money income earning power of black families was about the same in the middle of the 1970s as it was at the beginning of the decade and, perhaps, even a little bit less favorable. Whether or not this is a "backward" trend remains to be seen.

[9] Ibid.

3

THE ECONOMICS OF DISTRIBUTING FREE BREAD

Once upon a time there was a benevolent dictator who decided that no one in his country should be deprived of the basic necessities of life; so he decreed that henceforth bread would be free. Of course, the dictator expected that more poor people would get to eat bread after it became free. And for a little while the amount of bread consumed increased only modestly. But not for long. The quantity demanded at a zero price soon began to grow by leaps and bounds.

To meet this increased demand the dictator had many more bakeries built and had old ones expanded. Since his economy was already at full employment, the only way he could build and staff his bakeries was by withdrawing labor and equipment from the production of shoes, houses, and other goods. The prices of these other goods went up accordingly, because their supply was reduced.

When the consumption of bread reached 100 loaves a day for every man, woman, and child in his domain, the kindly dictator decided to find out where all the bread was going. He was at his neighborhood bakery the next morning when it opened. A man in overalls backed his truck up to the bakery and said, "Fill it up." He then took three more loaves of bread, put them in the cab of his truck and drove off. Following the man until he reached his farm, the ruler saw him take the three loaves into the kitchen and then feed the truckload of bread to his chickens.

The ending of the story is lost in the mists of time, but we do recall that the dictator was warmly beloved by the country's chicken farmers, who erected a statue in his honor.

The parable of free bread should be familiar, since earlier chapters have discussed the economic implications of free clams, free parks, free fishing, and even free medical care. But our primary interest in those chapters was the effect of a zero price on resource allocation. Here, we want to examine the effect upon income distribution.

If the price of a commodity is kept artificially high by monopolistic restrictions, then people will buy less of it than they would if competition were restored and the price were lower. Similarly, if the price is kept below the competitive equilibrium, people will buy more than they would at the competitive equilibrium price. How much less or more in each case depends upon the elasticity of demand for the product. In the case of clams, parks, and other such free goods, the demand is elastic enough so that it greatly exceeds the supply at a zero price. The result is the necessity of instituting some form of rationing. As noted in the chapter on clamming, this in effect makes people's subjective evaluation of queuing time very important. For it is on that basis that the decision is made whether to clam, to go to a park, etc. However, since richer people typically value their time more highly than do poorer people (since each group has a very different opportunity cost), the effect is to encourage relatively more use by lower-income groups.

The only way the government can eliminate rationing of "free" goods and still keep them "free" is to divert resources from other parts of the economy. But these diverted resources can then no longer be used by others. The additional free goods can no longer be called free.

When people talk of establishing free universal health care, they typically do not envision the possibility of unmeetable demands. Rather, it is assumed that supply will always equal demand. Since the demand for health care appears to be quite price elastic, the amount demanded at a zero price will certainly exceed any quantity demanded at current prices. If universal medical care is to be supplied to all who wish it, an enormous diversion of resources from other sectors of the economy will be needed. Moreover, if we were to try to minimize the cost of the increased supply by establishing a ceiling on doctors' incomes, we would be producing precisely the results described in the case of the Pernambuco Tramway (see Chapter 7). Doctors would migrate elsewhere and students would take up other occupations, as has happened in Britain.

It is granted that some solution must be found for the economic ills of a sector of our population. Is selective income distribution of the "free bread" variety really the answer? When free goods and services are established, the belief is being affirmed that we do not trust people to make the right judgment in spending their incomes.

And if the question comes up, "*What* income?" it might be pointed out that an alternative to free bread may be available in the form of some device for general income redistribution. One of these, the negative income tax proposal, is discussed in Chapter 33.

THE ECONOMICS OF ECOLOGY AND INCOME DISTRIBUTION

There are few more unsightly aspects to the urban environment than the jungle of poles and overhead wires that foul the typical cityscape. When we extend the term "pollution" to include visual pollution, overhead wires are a prime candidate for inclusion in this category. The solution is to place them underground, and this process is going on in many cities around the United States.

Typically, the relocating of arterial wiring is paid for by a general rate increase; but in residential areas, it is not uncommon for the citizens of an area who want this change to form a Local Improvement District (an LID), develop a plan, and submit it to the appropriate body for approval. Usually the utility company pays part of the cost and each lot owner pays a proportionate share of the rest (in Seattle, the ratio has been approximately 50–50). Placing wires underground in an already developed residential area is expensive, with the total amounting to as much as $1800 per lot. It is not surprising that this type of cost-sharing has tended to restrict most underground wiring to higher-income areas. However, since the share paid for by the utility company comes from the general income received from everyone's rates, while benefits accrue to the upper-income groups, such projects reflect a redistribution of income from poor to rich.

Two alternative options exist. We could insist that the lot owner pay the entire cost of placing wiring underground, in which case there would be no redistribution but also, probably, very little change. Or, we could let the utility company raise rates sufficiently to alter the wiring of the whole city, in which case everyone would pay. At a recent public hearing on the subject in Seattle, the head of the local utility company testified that such a program stretching over a 10-year period would necessitate a doubling of electricity rates. A rate increase bears more heavily on the poor because the percentage of their income that goes for electricity is typically greater than the percentage for the rich. Thus the consequence is again to impose a greater relative burden on the poor than the rich. Is the case of underground wiring different in its effects on income distribution from other solutions to environmental problems?

Before we attempt to answer this thorny question, we reiterate here a fact of which all readers should now be well aware. Every action has a cost. That is, every action involves some opportunity cost, whether or not this cost is explicitly stated or even understood by those incurring it. Since our world is one of limited resources, it is also a world of tradeoffs. In the underground-wiring example, we can trade off higher electric rates (or smaller amounts of income to spend on other things) for beauty (no overhead wires). Beauty does not come to us free of charge. When it is realized that every alternative course of action involves certain sets of costs, then it is time to ask, "Who will bear these costs?" We have already seen what happened in one case. We can now discuss others.

Many citizens are attempting to have forest areas preserved as pure wilderness, arguing that we should preserve as much of our *natural* ecology (as opposed to that made by humans) as possible. Preserving wilderness areas involves costs and benefits. The costs include less forest area for other purposes, such as camping grounds and logging. Who bears these costs?

People who like to camp (but not backpack) in the first case, and people who buy houses and other wood products,[1] in the second.

Although the reader can easily understand the first case, the second may not be so obvious. Look at it this way. When fewer forest areas are used for logging, then the supply of lumber is smaller than it would be otherwise.[2] With any given demand (schedule) the price of lumber is therefore higher than otherwise. So houses are more expensive.[3]

Now for the benefits. Wilderness-area preservation offers benefits to all those who like backpacking in the preserved area, and all those who can enjoy fishing and hunting there. Benefits are also bestowed upon those who do not themselves backpack, hunt, or fish, but would pay something to keep the wilderness for their children.

To determine what effect the saving of a natural ecology area has on the distribution of income broadly defined, we have therefore tried to discover, as always, who bears the costs and who obtains the benefits. This is usually an empirical question which can be answered only by examining relevant data. From limited studies that have been done, we can make a tentative conclusion about wilderness preservation. It has been found that backpackers are, in general, well educated and earn considerably more than the average. Thus the gains from that activity go to middle- and upper-income groups. As for who bears the costs, we know that campers (those with tents, trailers, and camper-trucks) are on average less well educated than backpackers and earn considerably less. Hence we are trading off recreation facilities used by lower-income people in favor of those used by higher-income people.

As for the increased price of housing due to less lumber, we

[1] Or wood-product substitutes, for that matter.
[2] The supply schedule is farther to the left.
[3] Note that the same is also true for nonwood houses. Since the price of wood houses is higher than otherwise, more people substitute nonwood houses—and their price is bid up (their demand schedule shifts outward to the right).

know that the poor will suffer more than the rich, because housing expenditures are a larger fraction of the poor's budget.

We can easily take other examples. Question: Should the level of a dam be raised to provide more hydroelectric power, or should the virgin timber area around it be left a wilderness area for backpackers? As economists, we cannot answer the question. We can merely point out all of the costs and benefits associated with two (or more) alternatives. In this example the costs (in ecological terms) of raising the dam level would be borne largely by actual and potential backpackers. The benefits would be lower electricity rates and/or the saving of resources that would have been needed to develop an alternative source of energy supply. If electricity payments represent a larger fraction of the income of the poor than the rich, raising the level of the dam might redistribute income from the rich to the poor. We say "might," because the income is redistributed only if the poor pay less relative to what they get.

There is, of course, a way of preserving our ecology without redistributing income.[4] The government could institute user charges for such things as wilderness areas and hunting preserves, setting them to cover the imputed opportunity cost of the resources being used. The totals collected could then be redistributed in a manner that would compensate those bearing the costs.

[4] But not without redistributing the use of resources.

THE ECONOMICS OF WELFARE AND THE ELIMINATION OF POVERTY

The elimination of poverty was an impossible dream in the world of Malthus, that dismal forecaster mentioned in Chapter 1. But as the United States became richer, the persistence of poverty in the midst of plenty became an anomalous situation.

What do we mean by poverty? We must be able to define it if we are going to be able to eliminate it. Back in the time of the Johnson administration, the poverty line was based on an income of $3000 (in 1959 purchasing power) for a family of four. This figure was then adjusted for variations in family size or over time for changes in the purchasing power of money. Using this base, it was discovered that 32 percent of Americans were poor in 1935, 23 percent in 1959, and the figure had fallen to 8 percent by 1977. Based on this trend of roughly a reduction of 1 percent per year, poverty would be eliminated relatively soon. Yet such a definition of poverty continues to remain unsatisfactory since it is not the absolute but the relative level of income that is perceived to cause poverty. Indeed, by the absolute standard, even the relatively poor in America are better off than those of average income in most other nations in the world. But setting an "acceptable" relative standard has turned out to be a more difficult problem to solve. Since we have been measuring the percentage of income received by the bottom 20 percent of income receivers, it has fluctuated from about $4\frac{1}{2}$ to $5\frac{1}{2}$ percent but has not increased significantly. In the light of the massive transfer payments of the past several decades, this figure may seem surprising and indeed, to some extent, is deceiving. In fiscal 1976, expenditures for social insurance programs alone came to $153 billion of which $76 billion was old-age survivors' disability insurance (OASDI). Unemployment insurance was another $16 billion. Expenditures directly for public assistance in that year totaled $17 billion, which included old-age assistance, aid to the blind, aid to the permanently and totally disabled, aid to families with dependent children, and general assistance.

Surely there is something drastically wrong if such massive transfers do not lead to an increase in the relative income of the poor. First of all, the figures may be quite misleading. The income of the bottom 20 percent of income receivers is cash and does not measure income in kind. When we add income in kind, the picture changes quite substantially. Income in kind includes food stamps, whose federal cost in fiscal 1977 was $6.1 billion, and other food programs such as subsidized meals for schoolchildren, Medicare and Medicaid, and subsidized housing for low-income groups. Starting in about the middle of the 1960s, such in-kind transfer programs have expanded at a rapid rate. When such in-kind transfers are counted as part of income, a dramatic change in the distribution of income figures results. It has been estimated that the bottom 20 percent of income earners actually receive something on the order of 12 percent of national income. That is, a doubling of what the Census Bureau *money* income figures show.[1]

Ironically then, the bottom 20 percent of income earners are actually enjoying a relatively higher standard of living than

[1] Edgar K. Browning, "The Trend Toward Equality in the Distribution of Net Income," *Southern Economic Journal*, July 1976.

ever before, yet the U.S. Census Bureau has shown an increase in the poverty rolls. In 1975, for example, there was a 2.5 million person increase in the number of individuals officially defined as poor. Note that the government-defined poverty level in that year of $5500 for a nonfarm family of four was applied only to money income. It ignored almost completely the in-kind transfers mentioned here.

Thus the problem may not be quite as difficult to resolve as it first appears; yet the "welfare mess" does appear to be an extraordinarily inefficient system. A major deficiency is that the real burden of much of the welfare mess really rests on the poor, who are subjected to endless queuing and questionnaires. The human indignities associated with interrogations to check people's eligibility, with investigations, and with still more waiting lines add a major psychic cost to being poor. For a long time the Aid for Families with Dependent Children program had provisions in it that actually discouraged the male heads of households from living with female heads of households. And, finally, the enormous bureaucracy associated with the program means that a substantial share of the total expenses for such welfare programs are eaten up in the bureaucratic federal and state structures rather than being passed along directly to the poor. Can we do better? No solution is ideal, and the problems are indeed complex. The first thing to recognize is that many of the poor are not really employable. They are the aged, the infirm, the mentally deficient, and children, and, therefore, any program must be able to reach groups that are not employable. Certainly, improvements in the labor market will help. Ending discrimination and providing full employment are obviously essential requirements, but beyond that to reach this residue of poverty a broad program must be realized. One such alternative is the negative income tax.

How would such a program work? Briefly, if it were instituted tomorrow, every citizen without exception would fill out an income tax return next April. But for any individual or family whose income fell below the poverty level, the "tax" would be paid *to* him by the U.S. Treasury instead of taken

from him. A most significant point differentiates this program
from public assistance or "relief": The taxpayer may *have* income, and still receive the tax benefit as an income supplement
necessary to raise his standard of living. He has, in short, an
incentive to work. The incentive is directly related to how
carefully designed the level of negative tax is. The effective
work effort a man or woman puts forth is no doubt related to
the rate at which the negative tax benefits fall as earnings rise.

This point can best be brought home by considering the extreme example where a "decent" income is decided upon and
all individuals are guaranteed that minimum level of income.
Suppose it is $7000 for a family of four. If this level of income
is guaranteed, the incentive to earn any income has been reduced significantly because the effective tax rate on any dollars
earned up to that guaranteed income of $7000 is one hundred
percent. That is to say, the family's disposable income does
not rise with any increase in the pretransfer income between
zero and $7000. In more technical terms, we say that the
marginal tax rate is one hundred percent because the transfer,
or gift, from the government is reduced dollar for dollar as any
pretransfer income is earned.

Clearly, in order to reduce the work disincentive effect of
this one hundred percent marginal tax rate, we must reduce
it to some lower figure, say, fifty percent. Hence, a family of
four would be guaranteed $7000 but would lose $1 of
transfer for every $2 earned. Hence, at an income level of
$14,000, no transfers would be given to the family at all. This
particular program does improve work incentives but is much
more costly than the simple guaranteed income situation first
discussed. It would also involve giving income transfers to
something like 85 million people. Additionally, this program
would require that the remaining taxpayers in the system, that
is, those with incomes above the break-even point (which in
the above example was $14,000 for a family of four), would
have to pay increased taxes. In other words, the marginal tax
rate of the nonrecipients of the negative income tax would
go up.

This problem would occur with any increased income re-distribution program. Several presidential contenders have suggested the use of demogrants, where each family would receive a certain grant from the government at the beginning of each year regardless of income. Let's say that that demogrant would be equal to one-half the average family income. If average family income in the U.S. were $16,000, then the demogrant to each family would be $8000. Of course, these demogrants must be paid by taxes, thus such a system of demogrants and taxes redistributes income from those with above average incomes to those with below average incomes. In such a scheme, the marginal tax rate on all families would be fifty percent. Empirical studies have shown that marginal tax rates of fifty percent or higher do have a significant work disincentive effect, both on those who are paying the tax and those who are receiving the proceeds in the form of a transfer. Apparently, additional redistribution within the United States will require marginal tax rates in excess of fifty percent. Whether or not the benefits of increased redistribution will outweigh the costs of further reducing people's desires to work is, of course, an empirical question. Moreover, if we were to shift to a straight negative income tax, or demogrant system, we would have to deal with the large cost involved in dismantling the present welfare system. It is not surprising, then, that some have maintained that politically and socially it would be easier to merely modify existing programs.

INDEX

78 79 80 9 8 7 6 5 4 3 2